MONTANA CELEBRITY COOKBOOK

compiled by
Susie Beaulaurier Graetz

for the benefit of
**Intermountain Children's Home
Helena, Montana**

published by
Montana Magazine

DEDICATION

In appreciation for their willingness to gamely try any new dish I serve, I would like to dedicate this book to Corey, Cody, Todd, Cjay and Kara, who over time have been subjected to a great many of my cooking experiments. They say they still love me, and I adore them.

ACKNOWLEDGEMENTS

A debt of gratitude to all the people who helped make the *Montana Celebrity Cookbook* a reality. A special thanks goes to the staffs of *Montana Magazine* and the Intermountain Children's Home for their support and expertise as well as to Kris Wilkinson who by way of her tireless dedication to the home, introduced me to this very special treatment center (and who would have been doing the cookbook with me if she hadn't started a new job!). Also a special thanks to Avis Anderson, Dave Ashley, Ginny Archdale, Evelyn Boswell, Bev Braig, Jan Brunk, Dan Burkhart, Becky Fonda, Suzie Judge, Laurie McGuane, Patty O. Murphy, Ellen MacMillan, Marilyn Olson, Ane Patterson and Niki Sliter who all went above and beyond the call of friendship to do research, contact and cajole celebrities, or to promote the cookbook.

Homes of Montana Stars

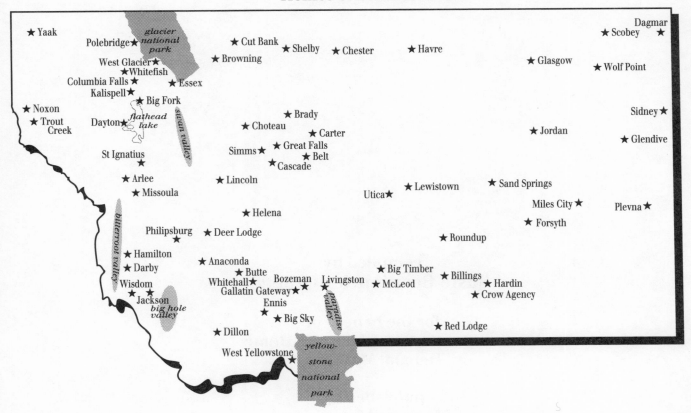

ISBN 1-56037-22-X

© 1992 American & World Geographic Publishing
P.O. Box 5630, Helena, MT 59604

INTRODUCTION

In the spirit of Montana neighborliness, you are invited to take a lighthearted peek into the personal recipe files of celebrities from all over the state of Montana as well as those who have strong ties to the Big Sky Country. Several of the recipes have been closely guarded secrets. Each has been printed much as it was received in the participant's own style and words.

Though I have been involved in fund-raising for the Intermountain Children's Home, I hate asking people for money. Asking for recipes was another matter, and so a celebrity cookbook seemed like the perfect project. The Intermountain Children's Home agreed and the project just took off.

Colleges and universities, local and national personalities, highly-visible Montana businesses, cowboys, artists, writers, athletes, Indian chiefs, actors, musicians, notable events and places, are just a few of the categories from which we drew. Time and the enormous range the book covers kept us from contacting more people. If you don't find your favorite celebrity here, please forgive me.

Of the nearly 300 people contacted, more than two thirds responded. Many sent donations along with their recipes. George Winston presented the Intermountain Children's Home with a collection of classic children's stories on video tape and cassette as well as his regrets for not being a cook.

Ted Turner and Jane Fonda sent their Black Bean Soup recipe even though they were in the middle of wedding and honeymoon plans. Jane apologized later after reading about some of the elaborate desserts in the book, for sending a "boring" (her words, not mine) recipe.

Autographed color posters of the Blue Angels flying team now decorate the walls at the Intermountain Children's Home thanks to Marine Captain Ken Switzer, and many notes were received commenting on what an honor it was to be asked to participate.

Some of our celebrities were reached in a round-about way. My friend Ellen MacMillan in Kalispell offered to help with Jack Nicklaus. Her husband is president of a bank and one of his employees often fished with Jack. The fishing guide passed the request to the managers at Jack's lodge and they in turn relayed the message to Mr. Nicklaus and we got our recipe.

Each recipe is a gift. We want to share them with you. May you find many pleasant surprises and wonderful meals inside.

Susie

Susie Beaulaurier Graetz

500 S. LAMBORN
HELENA, MONTANA 59601
PHONE 406/442-7920

JOHN H. WILKINSON
Administrator

SHARON HOWE
Director
Resource Development

This cookbook represents the goodwill and unselfish effort of an amazing cross section of our society. These well known and accomplished celebrities asked nothing in return for their contribution, and many wrote touching words about our project. Such signs of encouragement keep alive the faith that we can make life a little better for these deserving children.

The Intermountain Children's Home was founded in 1909 in the Helena valley and has been serving the special needs of Montana children and their families for more than eighty years.

Today, it is a residential treatment center for seriously emotionally disturbed children between the ages of 5 and 12. These are children who have been so abused (physically, sexually and emotionally) that they are no longer able to function in society. They have been "failures" in school, foster homes and other treatment centers.

We live with each of these children in family-like cottages, for an average of two years. We give every one of them intensive therapy, individualized education and the love and safety they have never known or been able to accept.

And it works. Eighty percent will be able to live with families once they leave the home. Our intensive program makes the Intermountain Children's Home one of the most effective treatment centers in the nation at working with severely disturbed children.

We have been fortunate to capture some national attention for it. A major article in the Los Angeles Times and a National Public Radio feature reported "good news" in treating these disturbed children. A Fox Broadcasting documentary team filmed in our home for three weeks in December of 1991.

Although we appreciate this exposure, what the Home needs most is continuing financial support. The Intermountain Children's Home is a non-profit organization that depends on private contributions for more than fifty percent of its operating costs. Helping these children is a difficult, expensive and people-intensive job; one we could not do without the steadfast support of churches, businesses and individuals who want to make a difference in the lives of children.

John H. Wilkinson

John H. Wilkinson
Administrator

CONTENTS

When I was growing up in Chester, I thought the Official State Fruit was Jello. So some of my Texas and Oakland friends smirk when I bring out my BBQ sauce.
Let 'em eat THIS! (on chicken, ribs, or burgers).

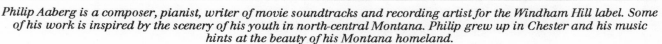

ROSE GARDEN PHIL'S UNIVERSAL BARBECUE SAUCE

3 Tbls. chopped onion
1 clove minced garlic
1/2 cup chopped celery w/leaves
2 Tbls. butter/margerine
4 Tbls. brown sugar
1 Tbls. Woochestershershire (sp.) sauce
1/4 cup or more lemon juice
2 Tbls. vinegar
1/4 to 1/2 cup blackstrap molasses
1 cup ketchup
1 tsp. dry mustard
1 tsp. (more or less according to tolerance) TOBASCO
1/2 tsp. liquid smoke
1/2 tsp. garlic powder
1/4 tsp. ground cloves
1/2 tsp. ground ginger
1/2 of a Hershey's milk chocolate bar
salt and pepper to taste

Melt butter/marg. in skillet.
Cook onions, garlic, and celery until translucent.
Add remainder of ingredients and simmer at least 20 minutes.

Options:
        -substitute tomato sauce for ketchup
        - add 1/2 cup red wine
        - add 1/4 to 1/2 tsp. cayenne/red pepper
        - if you like a thinner sauce, add some beer

Don't put the sauce on chicken or meat until it's already barbecued. Baste the meat with olive or corn oil to keep it from drying out while barbecuing.

Philip Aaberg

Philip Aaberg

Philip Aaberg is a composer, pianist, writer of movie soundtracks and recording artist for the Windham Hill label. Some of his work is inspired by the scenery of his youth in north-central Montana. Philip grew up in Chester and his music hints at the beauty of his Montana homeland.

 **Lockheed**

Gypsy Delight or "Egg-in-a-frame"

I was born in Fergus County, Montana, where my dad raised Aberdeen Angus cattle on a spread south of Lewistown. Through the sixth grade my school was a wooden schoolhouse with a fenced one-acre schoolyard, Mountain View District #129. The school never had very many students--I recall one year we had 8 pupils, one in each grade! Several of us rode our ponies to school and turned them loose in the school yard during the day.

My parents placed a high value on education and learning. They subscribed to the childrens' periodical <u>Childrens' Activities</u> for the benefit of us kids. I was always a book worm and read every issue through cover to cover. The only thing that has stuck with me all the years since from that magazine is the following recipe for the inexplicably named, *Gypsy Delight*. I still prepare these every Saturday morning for my wife, Evelyn (a Montana girl from Bozeman) and myself. My only innovation is the sprinkle of Louisiana Hot Sauce, a favorite of mine that we buy in quantity. In fact, when I flew on Challenger 8 in 1985 a little portion of this hot sauce came along in a plastic squeeze bottle for me to use on my freeze-dried scrambled eggs--the first hot sauce to fly in space!

For each serving:

1 pat of butter
1 slice of some interesting variety of bread
1 fresh egg

Put butter in a frying pan and heat it up to egg-frying temperature.
Cut a hole in center of the slice of bread, big enough to receive the egg.
   (I use the rim of a small juice glass as a cutter to make a nice round hole.)
Lay the bread in the frying pan until it starts to brown.
Remove the plug and break the egg into the hole.
Fry a bit and then turn gypsy delight over (turn plug, too).
Salt and pepper to taste.
Fry on second side until egg is done to your taste, it doesn't take very long.
Serve up with plug perched on top of the egg and a glass of orange juice on the side.
Sprinkle on gen-u-wine Louisiana Hot Sauce (generously!?!)
Enjoy!!!!

Loren W. Acton

Loren W. Acton

Loren Acton is Montana's first home-grown astronaut. He was raised near Lewistown, graduated from Montana State University and now works as a solar astronomer for Lockheed in Palo Alto, California. Loren was on the Challenger VIII mission in 1985.

CAMILLA M. ANDERSON, M.D.
405 WEST MAIN STREET
SIDNEY, MONTANA 59270

TELEPHONE: 406-482-1214

F R I K A D I L L A R   (Danish Meat Dish).

Coming straight from Denmark to Sidney-stagestop in Montana Territory six mos. before Montana became a state in 1889, enabled my parents with their three kids to share their Old World values with others - chief of which was frugality, and close behind that was warm hospitality and good tasting food. It was therefore natural that I learned about Frikadillar as soon as I was able to handle "solid food". It has never to my knowledge been declared Denmark's # One food, but I have never met a Dane who was a stranger to it. Of course it is a relative of American Hamburgers and Swedish Meatballs, but so much better tasting and more versatile.

I have never known anyone to have or use a recipe for Frikadillar, because the quantity of each ingredient is "a movable feast", and can be "extended" whenever one has an unexpected guest or two. Nor does one have to dread surprise guests or have to run to the store to buy the "makings", for what is needed is to be found in one's own kitchen. And it requires no special equipment or time for preparation, for it is always "as easy as pie" - a good "hurry-up" meal - winter or summer, and if there are left-overs, when these are sliced they make excellent filling for sandwiches.

Combine in fairly large mixing bowl:

Regular Ground Beef	1 to 1½ lbs
Pork Sausage	¼ to ⅓ lbs
Eggs	1 lrg or 2 small
Onion, chopped	½ to 2/3 cups
Flour	1½ to 2 heaping Tbs.
Milk, whole or 2%	½ to 2/3 cups
Pepper	¼ to ½ tsp.
Salt	½ to 1 tsp.

Frying time 9-15 mins.-Makes 12-15 Frikadillar - 1 to 3 per serving

Mix thoroughly, with spoon;
If there is plenty of time, let stand in refrigerator an hour or two.
    If time is short, fry promptly.
    The mixture will be relatively firm, homogeneous and not "runny".
Spoon a heaping Tbs. mixture to medium hot skillet, until pan is covered.
Flatten "ball" in pan with back of spoon until it is about 1/3 to ½ in.
    thick and round to oblong in shape.
Brown thoroughly on one side, then with spatula turn it over to brown on
    other side; do the same for each "ball."
When each one is done (browned and cooked through) transfer to serving dish.
Est snd enjoy.

Camilla M. Anderson

Dr. Camilla Anderson was born in Sidney in 1904, 15 years after her parents had come to Montana. She received her medical degree in 1929 and embarked on a career in psychiatry. Dr. Anderson has written five books on psychiatry and psychotherapy and is finishing her sixth book, an autobiography.

Veal Marsala

5 ounces of veal leg slice, pounded
2 ounces Marsala wine
1 tsp. shallots, chopped
2 pieces sundried tomatoes, oil packed, cut into strips
2 cloves roasted garlic
2 ounces veal stock
2 tsp. butter, cold
salt and pepper to taste

Saute veal in oil until browned on one side, turn over and brown on second side. Remove veal from pan and hold warm. Add shallots, roasted garlic and sundried tomatoes. Add marsala and reduce by half. Add veal stock and reduce by half. Whisk in butter and season with salt and pepper. Return veal to pan to rewarm. Transfer veal to serving plate. Spoon sauce over top of veal. Serve with pasta tossed in olive oil and fresh herbs, accompany with a fresh vegetable of your choice.
Serves one.

Bon Appetitto!

Chef Steven Nusbaum Toll

Andiamo is located in the Big Sky Resort. This intimate restaurant serves gourmet Italian dishes with flair.

When I was a youngster my Auntie Gloria came to live with me and my family. Auntie Gloria was just ten years older than me, so it was easy to relate to her. One day she took the bus into downtown Miami to go to Woolworth's to buy some mascara. Upon arriving at home she realized that she had left her package on the bus. She began to cry boo hoo boo hoo, I lost my mascara. Sooo, being a good nephew, I tried to think of something to do to cheer her up. I cooked her some pork chops, which anyone who knows me will tell you is my most favorite food, next to Chinese....Well, those pork chops have evolved into today's:

Pork Chops Auntie Gloria
Pork chops
Orange juice to cover
Soy sauce to taste (I prefer Kikkoman)
Garlic powder
Coleman's dry mustard
Coarse black pepper

Marinate chops a few hours in juice and soy sauce. Wipe dry and then coat with dry mustard, sprinkle with lots of garlic and black pepper. cook on a hot grill for a few minutes, then turn and sprinkle with more garlic and pepper.

Hope you enjoy!

Stu

Stu Apte is one of the world's most famous saltwater fly fishermen. He holds 38 saltwater flyrod and light tackle records. Stu and his wife, Bernice, have a home in the Gallatin Valley.

CHINESE HOT DISH

1 lb. ground beef	1 can chicken rice soup
2 Tbs. fat	1 can water
1 cup finely chopped onion	4 Tbs. soy sauce
½ cup washed uncooked rice	1 cup finely diced celery
	½ pkg. frozen peas

Brown meat in fat; add chopped onion and cook until golden and transparent. Add rice, soup, water and soy sauce. Place in 2 quart covered casserole and bake in 400 degree oven for 1 hour. During the last twenty minutes, add 1 cup finely diced celery and ½ pkg. frozen peas. More liquid may be needed.

This one-dish meal is a favorite with our family. Hot biscuits and a tossed green salad make this a delicious, nutritious dinner. We often serve it on Christmas Eve at our home.

Norma Ashby

Norma Ashby is best known for her award-winning television show, Today in Montana, *which ran for more than 22 years. Born in Helena, Norma is now a team manager for Mary Kay Cosmetics and lives in Great Falls.*

Mother Selma's Early Morning Dynamite: Standard fare before school during the depression years...

Take three potatoes and cook them for a half an hour the night before on the back of the stove.

Next morning take a medium sized onion, put it into a frying pan and sautee in butter until the slices are transparent like a frosty morning window pane.

Go back to the potatoes and slice into silver dollar sized slices. Put them in the pan. Toss them with finesse.

Break an egg into it. Add salt and pepper. Toss some. Share with your big sister...

Rudy Autio

Rudy Autio

I'm not much of a cook — but here's a favorite in line with my skills.

Rudy Autio is an internationally-known sculptor and artist who grew up in Butte and now makes Missoula his home.

**Babcock-Hauser Mansion
1885**

Mrs. Tim Babcock

720 Madison

Helena, Montana 59601

(406) 442-5611

HOT BEAN SALAD

2 SLICES OF BACON
1 ONION CHOPPED AND FRIED
1 CUP CANNED GREEN BEANS
1 POUND PORK AND BEANS
1 CUP KIDNEY BEANS
1 CUP BUTTER BEANS

YOU CAN ADD MORE BEANS OR SUBSTITUTE ANY OF
THEM EXCEPT THE PORK & BEANS.

1 CUP CATSUP
1 CUP BROWN SUGAR
3 TABLESPOONS VINEGAR
¼ TEASPOON SALT
1 TEASPOON DRY MUSTARD
1 TEASPOON WORCESTER SAUCE

MIX THOROUGHLY BUT GENTLY. BAKE IN GREASED
PAN OR CASSEROLE AT 325° FOR ONE HOUR.

Most sincerely,

Betty Babcock

---

*Tim Babcock was governor of Montana from 1962 through 1969. He has been a successful businessman in trucking,
ranching, motel operation and broadcasting. Tim and his wife, Betty, grew up and met in Glendive. They currently
live in Helena in the mansion built by Samuel Hauser, a territorial governor.*

JEFF BALLARD
Pitcher - Major League Baseball - Baltimore Orioles/St. Louis Cardinals

CHICKEN PESTO

1 packet of Knorr's Pesto mix
2 boneless breast of chicken
1/4-1/2 c. olive oil
1 clove garlic
1 - 6 oz. jar of artichoke hearts
1/2 c. pinon nuts (pine nuts)
1 - 10 oz. package of angel hair pasta

Grill the chicken breasts then cut into small chunks. Dice the clove of garlic and saute with the olive oil in a skillet. Add the pesto mix and complete the directions on the back of the Knorr's packet to make pesto. Cut the artichoke hearts into small chunks, add along with the grilled chicken and to the skillet with the pesto. Stir to mix. Cook the pasta according to the directions on the package. Drain the pasta, then add the pesto mixture to the pasta, toss. Serve immediately topped with a sprinkling of pine nuts.

I found the recipe in Cleveland while on the road playing the Indians. I decided since I like it so much and it is loaded with carbohydrates, that it would make a great pre-game meal. So now I commonly cook this the afternoon before I pitch.

Jeff Ballard is a major league baseball pitcher who was born and raised in Billings. He has played in the major leagues since 1987 and in 1992 signed with the St. Louis Cardinals. He returns to Billings every year during the off-season.

MILLER W. BARBER, JR.

MEXICALI SALAD

DRESSING:

    1   large ripe avocado, mashed
    ½   cup sour cream
    2   tablespoons Italian dressing
    1   teaspoon minced onion
    3/4 teaspoon chili powder
    ¼   teaspoon salt

SALAD:

    2   cups shredded lettuce
    1   15-ounce can kidney beans, drained
    2   medium tomatoes, chopped
    2   tablespoons green chiles, chopped
    ½   cup chopped black olives
    1   cup grated Cheddar Cheese, divided
    ½   cup crushed corn chips
         Picante sauce to taste

1. Combine ingredients for dressing and set aside

2. Toss together lettuce, beans, tomatoes, chiles and olives.
   Salad may be prepared ahead of time to this point.

3. Just before serving, layer lettuce mixture, dressing, picante,
   half the cheese, corn chips and remaining cheese in a large
   bowl.

Serves 4 to 6.

- -

I enjoy this salad with a big bowl of chili on a cold winter
day. A fire in the fireplace and a football game on the TV.

Pro golfer Miller Barber ranks third all-time in combined regular and senior PGA Tour earnings and is the only man to have won three U.S. Senior Open titles. He owns a cabin on Rock Creek and is part owner of Streamside Angler in Missoula.

First State Bank
of Shelby
DRAWER N
SHELBY, MONTANA 59474

SOUR CREAM CINNAMON BUNS

1 Cup dairy sour cream
2 Tbsp. butter
3 Tbsp. sugar
1/8 tsp. soda
½ tsp. salt
1 large egg
1 cake yeast
3 Cups sifted flour
2 Tbsp. soft butter
½ Cup brown sugar
2 tsps. cinnamon
1½ Cups powdered sugar
3 Tbsp. milk

In large pan, heat sour cream to lukewarm; stir in butter, sugar, soda, salt. Add egg and crumble in yeast; blend. Add half the flour, beat till smooth. Add remaining flour to make sticky dough. Dump onto lightly floured board; knead a few seconds to make smooth ball. Cover with bowl, let rest 5 minutes.

Roll out dough into 6 x 18" rectangle. Spread with soft butter, sprinkle on brown sugar & cinnamon. Roll up beginning at wide end; seal by pinching edges. Cut into 12 1½" slices. Place slices, cut side up, in well-greased muffin tins. Cover with damp cloth; let rise in warm place till light, about 45 minutes. Bake at 375° for 12 to 15 minutes. These buns may bubble over during baking. Remove at once from pan, put on rack. Frost while warm.

"The Star of the Meal"

Theo F. Bartschi
465 Judy Ave.
Shelby, MT 59474

—— 11 ——

MAX BAUCUS
MONTANA

WASHINGTON, DC
(202) 224-2651

MONTANA TOLL FREE NUMBER
1-800-332-6106

United States Senate

WASHINGTON, DC 20510

HUCKLEBERRY PIE

The "secret" in this recipe is, of course, the special ingredients which can only come from mountainous elevations; and the best are found in Montana!

The list of needed items is short: huckleberries--as many as possible of these bittersweet, blue-black wild fruit; sugar or honey; a tablespoon or two of flour; a pie shell; and butter to dot over all liberally. Then an oven for baking; 30 to 40 minutes at 350 degrees.

The taste comes with the eating, but even more so if the person who makes and eats the pie was in on the collection of the berries.

So splendid and rare a taste they are that black, brown and even grizzly bears treasure them and a person may run interference with one or more of these massive creatures when the season is at its height.

Wardrobe is important, too, and the company one chooses. Always include a foul-weather slicker, in a bright color and a rainhat and heavy boots for climbing. Part of the fun is hiking with friends and picnicking in a lovely glen. The remainder of the fun is in filling the buckets and then dumping each one into a larger group pot at central locations.

At the end of the afternoon, carrying home the precious and painfully-acquired berries to be divided up among all--and eventually into pies. Best of all is baking one immediately, for a sort of instant reward, although the berries can be put into plastic bags and stored in the refrigerator or the freezer. This guarantees that a good pie is a good memory and not just another meal.

Enjoy!

Max Baucus

Max Baucus was born in Helena, practiced law in Missoula and was elected to the U.S. Senate in 1979. His family has a ranch near Helena.

BILLINGS ROYALS AMERICAN LEGION BASEBALL

BY ED BAYNE, COACH

CHICKEN SPECTACULAR

3 cups	Cooked Chicken.
1 pkg.	Uncle Ben's Wild & White Rice, Cooked.
1 can	Cream of Celery Soup.
1 med. jar	Sliced Pimentos.
1 med.	Onion, Chopped
2 cups	French Style Green Beans, Drained.
1 cup	Mayonnaise.
1 can	Water Chestnuts.
	Salt and Pepper to Taste.

Mix all ingredients. Pour into a 2 1/2 or 3 qt. casserole. Bake 25 to 30 minutes at 350 degrees. Serves 16. Do not cook prior to freezing.

{ A truly spectacular and easy meal that has been made by our family on many nights before and after a late baseball game. Blueberry Salad goes great with the Chicken Spectacular. }

BLUEBERRY SALAD

2 pkgs.	Black Cherry Jello (3 oz.). Dissolve in 2 cups boiling water.
1 can	Blueberries (15 oz.) reserve juice.
1 can	Pineapple crushed (15 oz.) reserve juice. Add 1 1/2 cups of juice to jello mixture. Start to gel. Add fruit and set.

TOPPING

1 ctn.	Sour Cream (8 oz.).
1 lg. pkg.	Cream Cheese.
2/3 cups	Sugar.
1 tsp.	Vanilla.

Beat all ingredients together. Pour on jello. Top with crushed pecans or walnuts.

P.S. This Chicken Casserole is the one that really goes over great with all Baseball Coaches — young + old and all hope my wife will have it when they come to dinner. Ed Bayne Billings, Mont.

Ed Bayne has coached the Billings American Legion Baseball Team to 24 state championships in his 30-year coaching career. He has guided four teams to the American Legion World Series and has a career record of 1,243 wins and 319 losses. He has devoted his life to young baseball players in Billings.

DONALD E. THOMSON
Producer

I've spent a lifetime trying to convince people that I am not the domestic type. So when I was invited to share a favorite recipe to raise funds for the Intermountain Children's Home, my first reaction was to steal a line from another cookbook, "Every house should have a dog." However, there is one or two things I can do. If I've over-drawn the bank account, run over the dog, wrecked the car or any other offence that wives do to enflame their husbands, serving my huckleberry pie makes all boo-boos alright.

Huckleberry Pie

2 cups white flour
1 teaspoon salt
2/3 cup lard
3 cups huckleberries (fresh or frozen)
1 cup sugar
6-8 tablespoons flour
(You can add more flour or less depending on preference for runny or solid pie)

Heat oven to 425°

Pour huckleberries into medium bowl and toss sugar and 6-8 tablespoons flour with them (gently) until all berries are covered. Set aside and make pastry.

In medium bowl mix 2 cups flour, salt and lard, using two knives or any other pastry blender. I always do it with my fingers, squeezing the lard into the flour mixture until it's all crumbled and looks like cornmeal. (Wash hands first) Add about 8 tablespoons of ice water, tossing gently with a fork until it sticks together and can be rolled out. (Add more water to make it stick, a little at a time.) Roll out ½ of the dough on a floured, flat surface. Place on bottom of pie pan and fill with huckleberry mixture. Roll remaining dough and put on top of pie. Seal the edges and crimp edges in decorative style. Put fork pricks in the center for air to escape. Bake for 45 to 50 minutes. Let cool completely.

Note: This always leaks, no matter how carefully you try to crimp the edges, so if you don't have an oven that cleans itself, put a lining of tinfoil under the pie to catch the spill.

Jude Thomson

BIG SKY OF MONTANA
Ski and Summer Resort

P.O. Box 1
Big Sky, Montana
59716

(406) 995-4211
Fax (406) 995-4860

National Reservations
(800) 548-4486

Montana Reservations
(800) 824-7767

Group/Convention Sales
(800) 548-8096

BOYNE USA RESORTS

Big Sky, MT
Boyne Mountain, MI
Boyne Highlands, MI
Brighton, UT

PECAN-BREADED CHICKEN BREASTS
WITH DIJON MUSTARD SAUCE

8 Tablespoons (1 stick) butter
3 Tablespoons dijon mustard
6 ounces pecans, finely ground (about 1½ cups)
8 skinless, boneless chicken breast halves, pounded to ¼ inch thickness
1 Tablespoon vegetable oil
2/3 cup sour cream
½ teaspoon salt
¼ teaspoon freshly ground pepper

1.) In small saucepan, melt 6 Tablespoons of the butter. Whisk in
    2 Tablespoons of the mustard. Until blended, scrape into a
    shallow dish. Place pecans in another shallow dish.

2.) Dip chicken first in butter mixture, then dredge in pecans to coat.

3.) In large frying pan, heat remaining 2 Tablespoons butter in oil
    over medium heat. Add chicken and cook 3 minutes a side until
    lightly browned and tender. Remove to a serving platter and
    cover with foil to keep warm.

4.) Discard all but 2 Tablespoons of fat from pan and reduce heat
    to low. Add sour cream. Whisk in remaining 1 Tablespoon mustard,
    salt and pepper. Blend well. Cook just until heated through;
    do not boil. Serve over chicken.

Serves 4.

THIS is OUR AFRICAN GREYS favorite
too!

Sarah Kircher

*Big Sky Resort. From expert to beginner, from knee-deep powder to packed runs, from the view of Lone Mountain Peak
(it's breathtaking) to the best in western hospitality, Montana's destination ski resort has it all.*

—— 15 ——

BILLINGS MUSTANGS
Pioneer Baseball Club

I DON'T COOK - BUT I **DO** BARBEQUE - I **HATE** CHICKEN AND AM
ALLERGIC TO SHRIMP - **BUT** MY WIFE PEGGY'S 6 "S" RECIPE RECEIVES
<u>RAVES</u> AND IS A SALAD FOR **ALL** SEASONS!!!

SIX "S" SALAD
(Splendid Summertime Sports Season Sunflower Seed Salad)

Lettuce - Bibb (1/2-1 Head)/Red Leaf(1 Head) - Any Combination
Spinach - 1 Bunch+
Large Red Onion or 1 Bunch Green Onions, sliced thin, using
    some green
Chinese Peapods, blanched (optional)
7 1/2 oz. jar Fischer's Sunflower Nut Meats, dry-roasted
1/2 c. Fresh Parsley, chopped

6-8 oz. Frozen Orange-Juice Concentrate)
1/2 c. + Mayonnaise   ) Whisk til smooth

Broccoli Flowerettes, fresh, cut small
2 cans Mandarin Oranges, well drained
Seasoned Chicken Strips - heated

Place Mandarin oranges in bottom of large salad bowl; add torn
lettuces, spinach; peapods; broccoli; parsley; onions, and
sunflower nuts. Cover. Chill.

Whisk mayo and orange juice concentrate; adjust flavorings -
keep a TART taste. Pour dressing to coat but not drench salad
just before serving. Toss. Serve topped with 3-4 hot
seasoned chicken strips for each serving.

Serve remaining dressing on the side. Can serve as a main
entree or side salad. Serves 6-8.

Optional: (May add one or more or substitute) Hard cooked
eggs, sprouts/bamboo shoots, cauliflower flowerettes,
olives/water chestnuts, cherry tomatoes/radishes, jicama,
sliced thin, bacon/other nuts.

Variations: Pineapple chunks & pineapple juice with mayo
and/or Orange Juice Concentrate or a combination of both.
Keep tart. Large Shrimp.

Very truly yours,

Robert W. "Bob" Wilson
President/General Manager

---

*The Billings Mustangs joined the Pioneer League in 1948. They have been affiliated with the
Cincinnati Reds since 1974.*

ATLANTA FALCONS

Mike's Magnificent Meatballs

During the season I eat dinner with my team-
mate Mike Ruether and his family every Wednesday.
Mike is an accomplished cook and collector of
cookbooks. For some reason we always went out or
had pizza delivered. I was giving Mike a bad time
about this fact and the next week he responded with
these tasty morsels. Enjoy!

1/2 pound	Ground Pork
1/2 pound	Ground Veal
1/2 pound	Ground Beef
1 tablespoon	Worcestershire Sauce
1/2 cup	Italian bread crumbs
1 teaspoon	Anchovy paste(optional)
3/4 cup	Diced Parmesan cheese
1 large	egg

*A pinch of parsley
*A pinch of oregano
* Hot sauce to taste
1/4 cup olive oil for frying

I never measure-so you may need a little more
or less of something. (We're football players not
chefs.) Combine all ingredients in large bowl and
mix well. Form into meatballs. Fry in skillet with
olive oil on all sides until done. You can also brown
and then finish by baking them in the oven.
Serve as appetizers or with spaghetti for a main
meal.

Guy Bingham

Guy Bingham
#65
Atlanta Falcons

---

*Guy Bingham played football for the University of Montana Grizzlies. After graduation, he played for the
New York Jets and the Atlanta Falcons. Guy also gives time and energy to many charities. In 1992, he
joined the Philadelphia Eagles.*

JOHN BOZEMAN'S
BISTRO
RESTAURANT and CATERING
242 EAST MAIN
BOZEMAN, MONTANA
406•587•4100

FRESH HALIBUT "INDIA HOUSE"

They came from an island of good cooking. It was nearly winter 1985, two years after Tyler Hill and I transformed a Mainstreet deli into a full service restaurant we named John Bozeman's Bistro. They left the restaurant-rich island of Nantucket for a holiday season of skiing the slopes and trails surrounding their "other" home of Bozeman, Montana. They were the kitchen and dining room staff of Nantucket's famous India House stopping off to visit family and friends on their way to four months in the Caribbean.

Chef Teeba, originally from the paradise island of Tortola, his assistant Michael Caracciolo, and pastry chef / India House Manager Theo Hicken-Ranieri spent some portion of each day in the Bistro kitchen sharing culinary ideas, teaching us new techniques, and expanding our pantry possibilities. It was truly the beginning of the Bistro's International approach to cooking--what we called way back in 1985: *World Cuisine.*

The following recipe comes from Caribbean chef Teeba, an Alaskan chef, and a chef of Greek heritage whose objective it was to create an entree flavored with a single element considered most palatable by each of the three chefs. Teeba, of course, chose *banana* for its exotic sweetness and rich texture; the Alaskan chose *fresh Halibut* for its clean ocean flavor and perfect white texture; the Greek chose *Feta cheese* for its ability to marry other flavors while maintaining its own individuality. A week does not go by at John Bozeman's Bistro without a request for *India House.*

The Recipe

four 6-ounce (3/4 inch thick) fresh halibut steaks
(fresh Ahi tuna or fresh salmon when fresh halibut not available)

2 ripening bananas (not overripe) peeled and sliced

1/2 cup crumbled feta cheese

1/4 cup chopped pineapple (optional Bistro addition)

16 sheets of filo dough

1/4 cup melted butter or vegetable oil spray (low fat)

On a dry preparation table lay out one sheet of filo, lightly brush with butter (or spray with vegetable oil). Repeat four layers high. Lay one halibut steak in center of filo. Spread one fourth of the feta cheese crumbles evenly over halibut. Cover halibut with banana slices. For a real tropical "zip," top modestly with pineapple. Now wrap it up long sides first and fold over ends. Seal with a brush of butter. Repeat with remaining halibut steaks. Space each package one inch apart in a shallow baking dish, brush tops with eggwash for golden sheen, and bake in a preheated 450 degree oven for 15 minutes.

We serve *India House* at John Bozeman's Bistro topped with a simple lemon buerre blanc (white wine and cream) sauce. My wife and I love to serve *India House* at home simply with fresh wedges of lime for squeezing over these aromatic packages of culinary pleasure. We also invariably crack open a bottle of crisp, fruity fume' (Mondavi '88) or a buttery smooth Chardonnay (Girgich Hills '87) when topping with a cream sauce.

Pius Ruby
Owner / Chef

John Bozeman's BISTRO
RESTAURANT and CATERING
242 EAST MAIN
BOZEMAN, MONTANA
406·587·4100

..As head soup creator at John Bozeman's Bistro, I have made over 35,000 gallons of tasty nutritious soup for clients, family, and friends. This particular soup is by far the most colorful, and flavorful soup in my repertoire.

This is my favorite soup year around, especially during annual big game hunts, and wild game feasts with good friends and hearty red wine. The secret to the deep, red color and extreme rich flavors is the combination of fresh beets and the flavorful antelope meat.

INGREDIENTS   WILD ANTELOPE BEET BORSCH

1 antelope front shoulder
5 qts water
3 cups good red wine
2TBSP quality beef paste
5 med. fresh beets
1/2 cup celery
1/2 cup onion
1/2 cup carrot
I fresh tomato chopped
8 sliced mushrooms
I TBSP Tomato paste
I cup chopped spinach
fresh black pepper to taste
I TBSP parsley
I TBSP cilantro
I cup cooked wild rice

Season and rub the antelope shoulder blade with fresh garlic, garlic salt, dried oregano, cumin, and chili powder. Brown the meat in olive oil on all sides in large skillet approximately I5 minutes. Add chopped onion and celery, and cook 5 minutes. Deglaze with 2 cups quality red wine. Transfer meat and liquid to large stock pot and add 5 quarts water and beef base. Simmer 2 1/2 hours. Add beets, tomatoes, carrots, mushrooms and I cup of wine. Simmer 45 minutes until beets are tender.

Remove meat from bone and add to soup. Now add tomato paste, fresh spinach, fresh black pepper, parsley, cilantro and I cup cooked wild rice, cook I0 minutes and remove from heat.

Prior to serving add a dollop of yogurt or sour cream to each serving. One last detail.Guests traditionally add a spoonful of red wine from their glass prior to the first bite. Now relax and enjoy!

Tyler Hill

Tyler Hill
Proprietor and Chef

The Bistro occupies Bozeman's oldest building on Main Street. Homemade soups, gourmet burgers and high-rise sandwiches are featured for lunch. Upscale creative dinners feature fresh seafood and unique red meat presentations. Dining at the Bistro is always an adventure.

One of the favorite pastimes of my family when I grew up in Missoula was picnics along the streams and rivers which surround that community. The highlight of each meal was my mother's macaroni salad. The recipe is simple, but of all the macaroni salads I've eaten over the years, this seems to me by far the best. Mom told me she got this recipe from my grandmother, who was born in Bannack in 1873, but other than that I can't trace its ancestry.

MACARONI SALAD

1 lb (2 3/4 c) salad macaroni - cooked
1 cup chopped celery
1/2 cup chopped onions
1 cup chopped cabbage
3 pimentos
2 hard boiled eggs - chopped
salt

Mix with salad dressing and let stand before serving. Makes a large salad which gets better and better the longer it stands.

Alan Cain

Alan Cain

Blue Shield was founded as Montana Physicians Service in 1940. Blue Cross was founded as Hospital Service Association of Montana in 1946. In 1986 these two services merged into the Blue Cross Blue Shield insurance company we know today.

FOREVER WILD ENDOWMENT

Schaum Torte - directly translated as a Cake of Foam - was prepared only for festive occasions in our home. An endowment from old German ancestry it was always associated with some celebration at our home, a special treat for special occasions. It was a great favorite of mine. It would melt in your mouth. I was delighted when my mother, recognizing my wife's exceptional culinary talent as well as the frequency of special occasions in our home, chose to leave Helen the special pan in which it must be baked. After all, I had a sister and three brothers all older than me and it seemed they always had higher priorities than I did. The spring pan can be disassembled when the torte is done. Otherwise it would be extremely difficult, perhaps disastrous, to try and remove it as ordinary cakes are. Helen claims that it is not all that difficult to make, but nevertheless, we have it only on festive occasions, carrying forward the old family tradition. Try it. It adds that special touch to special occasions. An Endowment for us all.

Schaum Torte

6 egg whites
1/2 tsp Cream of Tartar
2 cups sugar
1 T vinegar
1 tsp vanilla

Beat egg whites with the Cream of Tartar until stiff but not dry. Gradually add the sugar, slowly, one tablespoon at a time. When mixture is very thick, add 1 tablespoon vinegar and 1 teaspoon of vanilla. Put batter in a greased spring form pan. Bake for one hour at 275 degrees. Turn off oven and let Torte remain until oven cools. Serve with fresh fruit and whipped cream.

Arnold W. Bolle, Chairman

Arnold Bolle is a retired University of Montana Forestry dean whose lifelong commitment to conservation has been to promote the management of forests for their diversity of plant and animal life, scenic beauty, clean air and water, wildlife habitat and forage, and recreation as well as their timber. He lives in Missoula.

THE ULTIMATE BOP-A-BAR-B-QUE

After a long weekend of performing, we enjoy getting together with our families for a Sunday afternoon bar-b-que. These recipes are simple and quick to prepare and make for a great bar-b-que.

BURGER MIX

2 LBS. LEAN GROUND BEEF
1 WALLA WALLA SWEET ONION
1T GARLIC SALT
3 T A-1 STEAK SAUCE
2 EGGS

CHOP ONION TO FINE CONSISTENCY. COMBINE ALL INGREDIENTS AND MIX WELL. FORM INTO PATTIES OF 1/4 TO 1/2 LB. COOK AND SEASON AS DESIRED.

NOTE: FOR ADDED FLAVOR ADD 1/2 LB SPICY PORK SAUSAGE

CABBAGE RAMEN SALAD

2 BONELESS CHICKEN BREASTS CUBED
1 SMALL HEAD GREEN CABBAGE COARSELY CHOPPED
1 SMALL HEAD RED CABBAGE COARSELY CHOPPED
1 PACKAGE RAMEN NOODLES RAW AND CRUSHED
1 THICK SLICE OF ONION CHOPPED
SESAME SEEDS
SLIVERED ALMONDS
SWEET RICE VINEGAR
SALAD OIL
TERIYAKI SAUCE

MARINATE CHICKEN OVERNIGHT IN TERIYAKI. STIR FRY CHICKEN, THEN REFRIGERATE. COMBINE ALL INGREDIENTS INCLUDING CHICKEN AND EQUAL PARTS VINEGAR AND OIL (approximately 1 cup of each). IT IS BEST IF THE SALAD IS REFRIGERATED FOR SEVERAL HOURS BEFORE EATING. SEASON WITH SALT AND PEPPER TO TASTE.

POTATO SALAD

8-10 MEDIUM POTATOES
1 BUNCH GREEN ONIONS CHOPPED
1 DILL PICKLE FINELY CHOPPED
4 HARD BOILED EGGS SLICED
6 TO 8 STICKS CELERY FINELY CHOPPED
2 CUPS MIRACLE WHIP OR MAYO.
2T DURKEE SAUCE
2T PREPARED MUSTARD
1t TARRAGON
SEASONING SALT AND PEPPER TO TASTE

BOIL POTATOES TO SOFT CONSISTENCY. PEEL AND CUT INTO APPROXIMATELY 1 INCH SQUARES AND REFRIGERATE FOR 2 HOURS. COMBINE ALL INGREDIENTS EXCEPT POTATOES AND EGGS AND MIX WELL. THEN ADD CHILLED POTATOES AND EGGS AND SEASON TO TASTE. GARNISH WITH PAPRIKA.

PEACH JELLO DELIGHT

1 LARGE PACKAGE PEACH JELLO
2 CUPS VANILLA ICE CREAM
1 PINT WHIPPING CREAM
FRESH SLICED PEACHES

DILUTE JELLO IN 1 CUP OF BOILING WATER. THEN MIX

This is a simple bar-b-que recipe which should be a big hit.

The Bop-A-Dips formed in 1972. They play high-energy music of the 1950s and '60s, presented via costumes, comedy and crowd-pleasing talent. The six on-stage band members make their homes in Missoula.

I enjoy cooking ethnic foods and a delicious favorite of mine is from my Lebanise family heritage. This dish, which I have changed and modified over the years, is a perfect hot accompaniment for a roast leg of lamb dinner, or cold and sliced aesthetically for an hors d'oeuvre.

IMAM BAYILDI
(translated: The priest fainted)

STUFFED EGGPLANT WITH GARLIC AND OLIVE OIL

1 eggplant (about 1 1/4 lb.)
salt
1/2 cup highest quality extra virgin olive oil (Italian)
2 medium onions, chopped
3 medium ripe, juicy tomatoes, peeled and chopped (if impossible to find, use one medium can of tomatoes)
5 medium cloves of garlic, chopped (you may want more...I do!)
1/2 cup chopped parsley
2 tbs. chopped fresh mint leaves
1/2 cup water or juice from canned tomatoes
salt and pepper

cut.

Remove the stem and hull of the eggplant. Score and peel lengthwise in one inch strips, leaving one inch strips of skin in between, making a striped design. Make two lengthwise slashes in a V shape 1 inch deep and 1/2 inch apart through the peeled part.
Sprinkle with salt.
Let stand 30 minutes.
Rinse under running water.
Pat dry with paper towel.
In a heavy casserole heat 1/4 cup olive oil. Add the eggplant and fry until lightly and evenly browned on all sides.
In a separate bowl, combine the remaining 1/4 cup olive oil with onions, tomatoes, garlic, parsley, mint, and salt and pepper. Mix well.
Stuff the eggplant pockets with this mixture. Replace the eggplant in the casserole, add the water and spread any leftover stuffing on the top.
Bring to a boil and cover. Reduce heat to low and simmer 50 minutes or until tender, adding a little water if necessary.
Carefully lift from the post, arrange on a platter with extra sauce and parsley garnish around it. Enjoy!

dana boussard

Dana Boussard is a fiber-construction artist who uses primitive western symbols in her art that depict the people, land and environment of Montana. Her work hangs in public and private buildings across the U.S., in Canada, China and England. She is a native of Choteau and now lives in Arlee.

SUSAN AND JEFF BRIDGES

BREAD PUDDING

1 can sweetened condensed milk

3 cups hot water

Combine and pour over 2 cups finely diced bread crumbs. Let stand until lukewarm. Then add:

3 eggs slightly beaten

1 Tb. melted butter

1/2 tsp. salt

1 tsp. vanilla or 1tsp. grated lemon rind

Pour into greased 1 & 1/2 quart baking dish and place in a larger pan filled with hot water to depth of 1". Bake in a 350 degree oven until knife inserted comes out clean, about 1 hour. Serve hot or cold, with cream, fruit or preserves if you wish.

*   *   *

This bread pudding recipe was discovered by my mother-in-law, Dorothy Bridges, in the first apartment she and Lloyd shared in New York over Fifty years ago. It is a family favorite and just one of lifes' many sweet things that she has passed on to us.

Enjoy!
Susan Bridges

Jeff Bridges' big break came in The Last Picture Show *in 1971. A few years later he was introduced to Montana when he filmed two movies here,* Thunderbolt and Lightfoot *in 1974 in Great Falls and* Rancho Deluxe *in 1975 in Livingston. His latest movies have included* The Fabulous Baker Boys *and* The Fisher King. *He owns a home near Livingston.*

Meredith Auld Brokaw

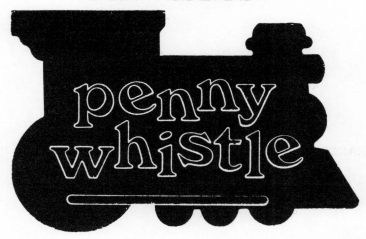

Chocolate Doggie Bisquits (for people, only)

from the <u>Penny</u> <u>Whistle</u> <u>Birthday</u> <u>Party</u> <u>Book</u> (to be published by Simon and Schuster Spring, 1992)

2 1/2 sticks margarine or butter, at room temp.
1 3/4 C. powdered sugar, sifted
1 large egg, at room temp.
2 1/2 C. all-purpose flour
1/2 C. unsweetened cocoa
1/4 tsp. salt

Cream butter and sugar in a mixing bowl with an electric mixer until light and fluffy, about 2 minutes. Mix in the egg, beating another minute. Add the flour, cocoa, and salt; mix until incorporated. Divide the dough into 3 parts. Flatten each into a disk and wrap in plastic wrap. Refrigerate until firm, at least one hour. The dough will keep for up to 5 days wrapped in plastic wrap in the refrigerator.

To bake, preheat oven to 325 degrees. Grease cookie sheet. Remove one disk of dough at a time from the refrigerator. Roll until approximately 1/8" thick. Remove top piece of plastic wrap and cut out your cookies using a doggie bone cookie cutter.*   Place on cookie sheet and bake for 10-12 minutes. *(These cookie cutters come in 4 sizes. You will produce 2 1/2 dz. cookies with the 4 1/2" size bone.)

Meredith Auld Brokaw, who owns a Boulder River ranch with husband Tom, is proprietor of five Penny Whistle toy stores in New York and author of four best-selling children's party-planning books. She is on the Board of Directors of Gannett Publishing, publishers of USA Today.

30 Rockefeller Plaza
New York, NY 10112
212 664-4214

A Division of
National Broadcasting
Company, Inc.

Tom Brokaw

GRANOLA

Makes 1 1/2 pounds

Ingredients-

pitted dates, prunes, or other fruit cut up
raisins
4 cups of old-fashioned oatmeal
1 cup shredded coconut
1 cup pine nuts or walnuts
1 cup wheat germ
1/3 cup sesame seeds
1/2 cup honey
1/2 cup oil

Mixing Procedure-

Snip dates into small pieces and set aside.
Combine oatmeal, coconut, nuts, wheat germ,
and sesame seeds in a large bowl.
Stir honey and oil in saucepan - heat to boil.
Stir honey/oil combination into oatmeal
mixture - mix well.
Spread new mixture into two 10 x 15 inch baking
pans.
Bake for 25 minutes at 325 degrees, stirring
occasionally - add fruit.

Tom Brokaw anchors the NBC Nightly News. *He and his wife, Meredith, own a ranch on the Boulder River south of Big Timber.*

EAST, INC.

JAMES R. BROWN, Director Aviation Programs

I found out after my triple by-pass that tastes, for the most part, are relative. I was lucky enough to hire on an enlisted aide who was a gourmet cook, by the name of TSgt Rey Olivo. Everything I eat is low cholesterol, low fat and I miss nothing in taste. We have a complete cookbook on this type of cooking and Rey was featured by one of the local TV/Radio stations for a Thanksgiving Dinner while we were still on active duty with the United States Air Force.

SAUTE LEMON CHICKEN

1. Preheat pan with 2 tablespoons oil, 1 tablespoon margarine, 1 clove garlic (crushed)

2. Flatten chicken breast and cut in half

3. Flour and put in to pan

4. Saute lightly

5. Remove chicken from pan

6. Add 2 ounces white wine at medium high heat

7. Add 1/4 teaspoon flour in to the pan to make a roux

8. Add 1 to 2 ounces of chicken stock

9. Add 1 ounce of lemon juice (fresh, if possible)

10. Add chicken and saute until gravy has reached desired thickness. If too thick, add more chicken stock

11. Serve on toast or linguine

12. Options: Add fresh mushrooms, touch of nutmeg or curry and serve over rice

James R. Brown

James R. Brown was a Lieutenant General in the United States Air Force. He was Commander of Allied Air Forces in Southern Europe and Deputy Commander in Chief U.S.A.F. for the Southern Europe Area. He retired as Vice Commander of Tactical Air Command, Langley Air Force Base. He was born in Bozeman and graduated from MSU.

NORTHERN AG NETWORK

P.O. BOX 1742 BILLINGS, MONTANA 59103
(406) 252-6661

"the powerful Voice of Northern Agriculture"

Easy Beef and Shrimp Kabobs

1 1/2 lbs. boneless top sirloin steak
1/3 cup soy sauce
2 tablespoons sugar
2 tablespoons water
1 tablespoon sherry extract
2 cloves garlic, minced

1 teaspoon grated ginger
8 whole large mushrooms
8 one-inch cubes pineapple
1 small green pepper
1 small onion
8 jumbo peeled shrimp

Combine soy sauce, sugar, water, sherry extract, garlic, and ginger root to make a marinade. Cut steak into sixteen 1 inch cubes, place beef with shrimp into plastic bag. pour marinade over beef and shrimp, turning to coat. Tie bag securely and marinate in refrigerator 6 to 8 hours (or overnight, if desired).

Drain marinade into small saucepan and cook slowly for 5 minutes. Slice onion and pepper into about eight pieces each. Alternately thread 4 beef cubes, 2 pineapple cubes, 2 green pepper pieces, 2 shrimp, 2 mushrooms, and 2 onion pieces on each of four 12-inch skewers.

Place kabobs on a barbeque grill so that the surface of the meat is 3 to 4 inches from heat. Broil 10 to 20 minutes, depending on the doneness desired for your steak, (rare to medium-well), turning kabobs over and brushing with marinade occasionally.

Makes four servings.

Note: I'm a beef lover, and we started using this recipe whenever we have dinner guests that we really want to impress! It's simple to fix and all the work can be done well ahead of time so all you have to do is drag the kabobs out of the refrigerator and stick them on the grill when you're ready to eat. For tasty hors d'oeurves, you can make up some smaller version of these kabobs on shorter skewers. Use high quality beef steak and with this marinade you'll have a treat that will melt in their mouth!

Taylor Brown

Taylor Brown

Taylor Brown, one of the nation's leaders in the field of agriculture broadcasting, grew up on a cattle ranch near Sand Springs. He is the owner and voice of the Northern Ag Network, which provides farm news and market information to radio and television stations. Taylor, his wife and family live near Billings.

P.O. BOX 279, BIG SKY, MT 59716
PHONE (406) 995-4111

It is with great pleasure that we pass on this Buck's T-4 Lodge traditional favorite recipe of Russian Cream with Raspberries. It has been a big hit with all of our customers visiting the beautiful Big Sky area. Enjoy!!

RUSSIAN CREAM WITH RASPBERRIES
(Serves 12)

4 1/2 CUPS WHIPPING CREAM
2 1/4 CUPS GRANULATED SUGAR
3/4 CUP WATER
1 T. GELATIN
33 OZ. SOURCREAM
2 tsp. VANILLA
2 PINTS. FROZEN OR FRESH RASPBERRIES

METHOD: HEAT WHIPPING CREAM WITH SUGAR, JUST HOT ENOUGH TO DISSOLVE SUGAR, DO NOT OVERHEAT. HEAT WATER IN SEPARATE PAN, ADD GELATIN AND DISSOLVE. ADD TO CREAM MIXTURE, WHIP IN SOURCREAM AND ADD VANILLA AND CHILL OVERNIGHT.

LAYER IN STEMMED WINE GLASSES WITH RASPBERRIES, TOP WITH FRESH WHIP CREAM IF DESIRED!

Buck's T-Four in Big Sky was established in 1946 as a hunting camp. It has developed into a full-service resort offering superb food, a night's lodging and some old-fashioned western hospitality. The menu specializes in wild game and Montana steaks.

United States Senate
WASHINGTON, DC 20510-2603

COMMITTEES:
COMMERCE, SCIENCE, AND
TRANSPORTATION
ENERGY AND NATURAL RESOURCES
SMALL BUSINESS
SPECIAL COMMITTEE ON AGING

This is my wife's recipe for Quick and Easy Taco Meatballs:

    2 pounds hamburger
    1/2 chopped onion
    2 eggs, slightly beaten
    1 package taco mix
    salt
    pepper
    garlic

    Mix together, form into small meatballs and place
on cookie sheet. Bake at 400 degrees for 15 minutes.

With best wishes,

Sincerely,

Conrad Burns
United States Senator

Conrad Burns is Montana's 19th United States Senator. In 1975 he created the Northern Ag Network, which he sold in 1986 before beginning his political career. Conrad and his wife, Phyllis, are from Billings.

This is an exotic dish that takes no more than 20 minutes to cook and has impressed such noted gourmands as the celebrated artist and trencherman, Russell Chatham. I generally hesitate to tell him that the recipe is adapted from Jane Brody's Good Food Book, as Chatham considers Ms. Brody to be a "Nutrition Ninny."

HOT SCECHUAN-TYPE NOODLES WITH PEANUT SAUCE
by Tim Cahill

Put the water on to boil 12 ounces of linguine. While the linguine is boiling make the sauce.

The Sauce:
Combine 1/3 cup hot water
        1/3 cup chunky peanut butter (preferably
            all natural)
        2 teaspoons soy sauce
        2 teaspoons rice vinegar or white wine
            vinegar
        5 cloves of garlic, finely minced
        2 teaspoons sugar
        1 to 4 teaspoons Hot Red Pepper flakes
            (or to taste)

Combine the sauce with the hot linguine in a serving bowl. Garnish with 2 tablespoons chopped scallions.

This dish can be served hot, room temperature, or cold.

Tim Cahill

Tim Cahill is co-founder of Outside Magazine *and author of* Jaguars Ripped My Flesh *and* Road Fever. *He writes travel and adventure articles.*

CARROLL COLLEGE

I enclose my recipe for Uncle Joe's Egg Nog. Besides being fattening and bad for the arteries, it's addictive. You can't take just one cup.

Uncle Joe's Egg Nog

by Matt Quinn

Ingredients:
1 doz eggs, 4 qts milk, 1 qt heavy cream, 4 tsp vanilla, 1/2 tbs nutmeg, 1+ cup sugar, 1/2 qt rum, 1/2 qt whiskey or brandy.

1.   separate eggs

2.   beat yolks well

3.   add vanilla, nutmeg and some sugar to 2

4.   beat cream till partially stiff

5.   add some sugar to 4

6.   add milk gradually to beaten yolks

7.   add beaten cream to 6

8.   stir thoroughly

9.   beat egg whites stiff and add rest of sugar

10.   add rum and whiskey or brandy to 8

11.   add egg whites to 10

12.   stir thoroughly and chill

Makes 6-7 quarts. Don't ask about calories or cholesterol.

Cordially,

Matthew J. Quinn, Ph.D., J.D.
President

Carroll College in Helena, a four-year, Catholic, liberal arts, co-ed college, was founded in 1909. The college has a strong tradition of academic excellence as shown by its 90 percent graduate school placement. Carroll is ranked third in the nation in its number of Truman Scholars, and its debate team is ranked first in the Northwest.

—— 32 ——

Camp Salad

This salad will guarantee regularity — a problem at times with cowboys. With all the beef & beans they eat this good salad helps keep the air sweet & fresh around cook houses & camps.

Actually, this recipe has been in our family for years — we stole it from the Thunderbird Country Club in Palm Springs. It was known locally as "Thunderbird Salad." My dad was a Thunderbird chef until his retirement & the recipe was developed by my mom & dad — really.

In 1975, I was painting & working on the Sun Ranch near Ennis & my parents took over the cook house chores. This salad was a real favorite with the crew & the salad is filling.

Gary Carter Jr

Salad Dressing
1/3 cup salad oil
2/3 cup vinegar (white wine vinegar)
1 tbsp. lemon juice
1 clove crushed garlic
1/2 tsp salt
1/3 tsp pepper

1/2 head lettuce cut fine
1 lrg tomatoe diced fine
1 avacado diced fine
3/4 cup chopped celery chop fine
1/3 cup chopped fine green onion
8 strips crumbled crisp bacon

Mix together in salad bowl & crumble 2/3 cup blue cheese on top of salad — pour dressing over salad & toss well —

Gary Carter is a cowboy, avid fisherman, horse breeder and talented sculptor and painter living near West Yellowstone. He was awarded a gold medal in 1990 for a drawing submitted to the elite Cowboy Artists of America, of which he is past president.

Original sketch by Gary Carter.

Russell Chatham

Post Office Box 990 ✳ *Livingston, Montana 59047* ✳ (406) 222-6957

UPLAND BIRD RISOTTO

This is my personal version of the classic Italian primi, or first course. One of the watermark examples of it was fixed for me a number of years ago by Peter Lewis, owner of the superb Campagne Restaurant in Seattle. Since then, I have varied it dozens of ways. What follows is the basic outline of this simple, yet remarkable dish.

The necessary wild mushrooms may be CEPs (called porcini in Italian, these are the preferred variety) or morels. Depending upon the altitude, rainfall and time of year, both can be picked in Montana.

Any number of birds will work: ruffed grouse, sharptail grouse, sage grouse, blue grouse, Hungarian partridge and pheasant. You can also use chukar or quail, though you'll have to shoot those in Idaho, Nevada, Oregon or Washington.

The quantity will depend on the number of people to be fed. Six seems ideal to me. Eight is probably the maximum if you consider the normal home kitchen with its normal utensils. You can use a standard cast iron Dutch oven, or an enameled, oven-proof casserole.

If you are cooking for eight—or six, for that matter—you'll need two huns, two chukars, four quail or one each of any of the other birds mentioned, except the sage grouse. If using the latter, it must be a very small yearling bird, or else leftovers from a previous meal.

Ingredients:
Chicken stock—about 4 cups. Homemade is preferred, but the low salt, store-bought kind will work.
Game stock—can only be homemade from the carcasses left over after numerous meals.
Dry Vermouth—about 1 cup
Onion
Butter
Olive oil—a flavorful variety is best
Salt
Pepper
Thyme
Parsley—fresh, Italian is best
Cheese—Reggiano Parmesan or aged Asiago
Rice—Italian arborio is preferred

To start, roast bird(s) in a 450° oven. If ruffed, sharptail, blue, small sage or pheasant, brown first in a hot skillet with a mixture of olive oil and butter (the smaller birds, huns, chukar or quail may also be browned, splashed with vermouth, and covered until done rare). Cook the larger birds not more than fifteen minutes to keep them rare. Set aside to cool. (Bird(s) can be prepared ahead of time if you wish). When cool, carve

off legs and breast. Partly cut, partly tear meat into small pieces, sized as you prefer (save the bones for stock!).

If you have a fire going to grill a main course, say, antelope loin or rack of lamb—perhaps with sweet Italian sausage on the side!—grill several slices of onion and set aside.

If your mushrooms are dried, which they most likely will be, soak them in warm water for at least an hour before using.

Twenty-five minutes before you want to eat, begin as follows:

Heat cooking pan over medium heat. Finely chop one onion and put in with a generous amount of olive oil and butter (about ⅔ oil to ⅓ butter). Cook until translucent.

Raise heat to medium high and add rice (do not rinse first). Stir rice into onion, oil and butter for six or seven minutes. Turn heat back down to medium.

Add the cup of vermouth, stir. As it evaporates, add a little chicken stock, about a half cup at a time (stock should be warm). As it is absorbed and as it evaporates, add more as you continually stir.

About halfway through the cooking time, about ten minutes, add the mushrooms. Add as well, the water in which the mushrooms were soaked. Stir until the liquid is absorbed.

Switching to the game stock, add one half cup at a time, continuing to stir. Do this for six or seven minutes. Add the pieces of shredded/cut-up bird. Keep adding game stock and stirring until rice is done. The dish should be very moist. Salt and pepper to taste. Add a few pinches of the thyme (fresh is best, but dried works).

Chop the grilled onion if you have it, and add this plus about one cup of the *freshly* grated cheese. Serve as individual portions. Garnish with the parsley.

Of prime importance in this dish is the sonorous blend of wild flavors, combined with its seductive, creamy texture. With this in mind, substitutions will not work. For instance, domestic mushrooms used in place of wild will negate the point of the dish, as will domestic grating cheese, especially the pregrated variety.

While I'm normally opposed to portion control, in this instance it is advised. Remember, this is a primi, a first course; your guests must still be able to approach their veal chop and spinach with enthusiasm. Therefore, serve their bowls for them with restraint, because if you don't they will launch into this irresistible delight to the point of exhaustion.

Any number of wines will work with this. Hold your Barolos or Bourguignonnes for the main course. Here you might want to try a Gavi, Pinot Grigio, or a Domaine Tempier Bandol Rose.

Russell Chatham has lived in Livingston since the spring of 1972. He has been a landscape painter for thirty-five years and a writer for twenty-five. He is also the founder and publisher of Clark City Press. He lives in Park County with his wife Suzanne, daughter Rebecca and son Paul.

CHICO
HOT SPRINGS LODGE
PRAY, MONTANA 59065
(406) 333-4933

Dennis Quaid came into the restaurant for dinner one night and asked if he could help cook. We weren't very busy so...no problem. Dennis wanted a Steak Au Poivre (pepper steak), but wanted to change our recipe a bit. I suggested that he leave his recipe in my hands and I'd prepare the steak his way. This is the result.

Steak Au Buck

2 Tenderloin medallions, 1" thick

Fresh crushed peppercorns

1 oz. Cognac

1 oz. Red wine

2 tsp. Fresh grated ginger

1 tsp. Fresh garlic

1 tbsp. Vegetable oil

2 tbsp. Pickapeppa Sauce*

2 tbsp. Demi-glace

Lemon juice from 2 wedges of lemon

Salt and pepper

Sliced mushrooms

Pack each side of the tenderloin medallions lightly with peppercorns.

Sear medallions in pan over high heat on each side for approximately 3 to 4 minutes, until medium rare.

Pull medallions from pan and set them aside. Add mushrooms to pan and cook for 2 minutes, then deglaze bottom of pan with spirits. Be careful of fire -- Cognac is very flammable. Add all other ingredients and reduce until slightly thickened. Pour sauce over medallions and serve.

This is a very spicy dish, full of many flavors.

* Pickapeppa Sauce is available at specialty stores and some grocery stores.

Marin Ganett

Chico Hot Springs was built in 1900 and is located near Pray in the Paradise Valley. Operated by Mike and Eve Art, Chico has one of Montana's premier dining rooms. Odorless hot pools, horses and a down-home, good-time, western bar round out this hotel's offerings.

Bill Christiansen for Lt. Governor Club

Box 314, Hardin, Montana

Phone: 406-665-1122

JOHN ANDREWS
State Campaign Chairman—Hardin

LARRY FASBENDER
Eastern District Chairman
Fort Shaw

GEORGE SHERWOOD
Western District Chairman
Missoula

PEG KOEBBE
Headquarters Chairman
Hardin

BOB SAUNDERS
Finance Chairman
Billings

Hattie and I find this recipe works well at our house because we have a large family (including 3 great-grandchildren!). This recipe is easy to double if we all get together on short notice.

Savory Baked Chicken

1/3 c.	margarine
1 1/2 c.	instant dry potatoes
1/3 c.	grated parmesan cheese
1/2 tsp.	salt
1	2 1/2 to 3 lb. chicken cut up
2	eggs beaten

Preheat oven to 400 degrees. Heat margarine in 9x13 pan in oven until melted. Mix dry instant potatoes, cheese and salt together. Dip chicken into eggs then roll in potatoes. Place chicken pieces, skin side up in pan. Bake uncovered until thickest pieces are done; about 1 hour.

Bill Christiansen is from Hardin and served eight years in the Montana House of Representatives. He was then elected to the Senate and named president of that body. In 1973, he was elected Lieutenant Governor. Bill is known for his involvement in numerous community services as well as statewide organizations. He and his wife, Hattie, live in Helena.

LAZY CHICKEN RECEIPT

Cooking time: 1 Hour - pre heat oven to 500 degrees.
1 Chicken about 2 1/2 to 3 lbs. (cut in pieces - 8 pieces)
3/4 lb. Small white or large yellow onion
1/2 lb. New potatoes or large potatoes
1/2 lb Carrots

2 Cloves garlic - crushed
1 tsp. Powdered thyme
3/4 tsp. Salt
1 Tbsp. Butter

1 Cup chicken stock
1/2 Cup dry white wine
Freshly ground black pepper
Chopped parsley for garnish

ART ORTENBERG
LIZ CLAIBORNE

1.)   Place cut up chicken skin side down in baking dish about 9 x 13.

2.)   Peel onions, if they are small, add them whole to the chicken. Add small new potatoes whole with skins, or peel and cut large potatoes in vertical quarters or chunks. Peel carrots, and again add ones whole or cut large ones into big 2" to 3" chunks. Tumble vegetables and chicken together so that pieces stick up a bit. Make sure chicken pieces are skin side down.

3.)   Sprinkle garlic, salt a generous amount of black pepper and powdered thyme over chicken and vegetables.

4.)   Pour in white wine and one cup of chicken stock. Chicken and vegetables should be half-covered by the combined liquids.

5.)   Dot chicken and vegetables with butter. Bake in upper third of pre-heated oven for between 50 minutes and 1 hour. Chicken and vegetables should brown as they become tender. Baste several times with pan juices, adding more chicken stock only if juices evaporate. Turn sections of chicken once so pieces brown on skin side. Allow 10 minutes extra time for browning under broiler if necessary.

6.)   Remove from oven and check pan juices. They should be reduced by about half. If not, carefully spoon off juices and reduce in a sauce pan. Pour back over chicken in the baking pan. Sprinkle generously with parsley and serve.

A cool green salad and some crusty, heated French or Italian bread, round this out nicely. (Yield 2 to 3 servings)

Use enameled cast iron pan - serve directly from the pan.

Liz Claiborne is a well known fashion designer. She and her husband, Art Ortenberg, now live on the shore of Lindbergh Lake and own a ranch at Canyon Creek. They are very involved in environmental issues.

CLEARY STUDIO
1804 Beltview
Helena, MT 59601
(406) 443-4535

PASTA WITH SALMON SAUCE

INGREDIENTS:

8 T olive oil, 1 1/2 t oregano, 1 t salt, 1/2 t fresh ground
pepper, 2 cloves garlic crushed, 1 t capers, 3 T lemon juice,
1 small onion chopped, 1/2 cu. water, 3 chicken bouillon cubes,
1/2 lb salmon filet with skin on, 4 T flour, abt. 3 cu milk,
1-4 oz. can mushrooms, 4 slices bacon chopped, Parmesan cheese to
taste and 16 oz. wide noodle pasta of choice (like Mostaccioli).

DIRECTIONS:

Saute onion and garlic in olive oil. Add salt, lemon juice,
pepper, capers, oregano and bacon. Cook for about 1
minute, add water, cook 1 min. Add fish skin side down and cover
and cook for 1/2 hour.

Carefully remove salmon to cool. Add 4 T flour to sauce and stir
until mixed. Slowly add 2 cups of milk (I use skim milk) and
stir until mixed. Add bouillon cubes and cook until dissolved
(about 5 minutes).

Skin, flake (and bone) salmon and add to sauce. Add small
drained can of mushrooms and cook about five minutes. Add up to
1 more cup milk if needed to thin. Serve over pasta with
parmesan cheese.

My husband is a fisherman who spends a week fishing for salmon in
Alaska in September and brings back a cooler full of his frozen
catch. I could only eat and cook so much poached and grilled
salmon before trying to invent a more creative way of using the
fish.

Shirley Cleary

Shirley Cleary is a noted award-winning and popular artist best known for her flyfishing scenes. Shirley lives in Helena.

35 W. Main
Bozeman, Montana 59715

I salute the Intermountain Children's Home and the people who make it possible. Because of their work, the terrible cycle of abuse and neglect and violence can be broken and the children who walk through their doors will learn what love is and have a chance for a viable future.

Glenn Close

Glenn Close

Gamoo's Baking Powder Biscuits

2 c.   flour
1/2 t. salt
4 t.   baking powder
1/2 t. cream of tartar
2 t.   sugar
1/2 c. shortening (butter is best, but margarine and
             even Crisco are possible)
2/3 c. milk

Heat oven to 425 degrees.
Sift flour, salt, baking powder, cream of tartar and sugar together. Cut in shortening until mixture resembles coarse crumbs. Add milk all at once and stir until dough follows fork around bowl. Pat or roll until 1/2 inch thick. Cut with biscuit cutter.
Bake on ungreased sheet for 10-12 minutes. They should be a lovely golden brown. Crisp on top and bottom but tender and flaky inside.

Some of my most treasured memories from childhood are the late Sunday afternoon high teas that my mother would prepare during the colder months. We would gather in the living room around 5 o'clock and, in front of a crackling fire, have homemade soup, scrambled eggs, crispy bacon and <u>always</u> these wonderful biscuits, still hot from the oven. My Mom would then read to us out loud, usually a ghost story from a battered old book that had belonged to her father.

Glenn Close is a Tony award winner and three-time Oscar nominee. She has appeared in films including The Big Chill, Fatal Attraction *and* Reversal of Fortune *and in 1992 won her second Tony, as Best Actress in* Death and the Maiden. *She owns a farmhouse outside of Bozeman and is co-owner of this Bozeman coffeehouse.*

CNN AMERICA, INC.
The CNN Building
820 First Street, N.E.
Washington, DC 20002
(202) 898-7900

During the Depression, seafood was for some reason one of the least expensive proteins available even in the States' interior (Wyoming and Montana) Herewith a casserole redolent of those good old bad old days.

(serves six)

1½ and a half lbs frozen cleaned shrimp

6 ounces crab meat

16 ounce pkg long grain wild rice

3 chopped green onions

1 tsp worcestershire sauce

1 cup mayonnaise

1 cup buttered bread crumbs

cook shrimp and rice as directed (using seasoning in rice pkg (uncle Ben's, probably)

mix all except bread crumbs and pour into 1 and a half quart casserole. Top with buttered bread crumbs. Bake at 350 for 20 to 30 minutes.

If times are good, you may substitute fresh shrimp and vein them yourself. If times are really good, you may toss in a piece of fried ham. I found the piece of ham once in a scalloped potato casserole in 1938, and it was a fairly good year.

Reid Collins

Reid Collins

Reid Collins, who began his career in Missoula, spent 20 years as a CBS correspondent and is now a Washington, D. C. anchor for CNN. Collins lived in Great Falls and Butte before attending the University of Montana.

Conrad Mansion Directors, Inc.
P.O. Box 1041 Kalispell, Mt 59903-1041

WILD DUCK OR GOOSE JERKY

Cut meat in strips or small pieces and marinade in YOSHIDA'S gourmet sauce for 24 hours.
Spread on a cookie sheet and bake at 150 degrees for 12 hours or until dry.
Cool and store in air tight bags if you can keep any around that long.

HUNTER'S CASSEROLE

An easy and versatile way to put a smile on your favorite hunter's face:

Cut a duck or goose into pieces (legs, thighs, breasts)
Place desired amount in casserole and cover with one of the following:
 Teriyaki sauce
 Mexican green salsa
 Sauerkraut
Bake at 300° for three to four hours or until the hunters return.
Keep moist by adding water or more sauce.
Serve with wild rice and steamed vegetables.

We selected a wild game recipe because Charles Conrad and his hunting companions Teddy Roosevelt and Jim Hill were avid sportsmen. We suppose the hunters simply sent their birds to the kitchen and Hori and his Japanese kitchen staff presented the dinner guests with a delicacy on a silver tray. In keeping with this fine tradition we have created recipes that are worthy of an elegant formal dinner, but are easy on the cook.

IMPORTANT NOTE: ONLY ACCEPT OVEN-READY BIRDS—NO HEADS, FEET OR FEATHERS!

Nikki Sliter

Nikki Sliter
Head Go-fer, Conrad Mansion Museum

The Conrad Mansion in Kalispell is a Norman-style mansion built in 1885 for the Charles E. Conrad family. It is three stories tall, has 22 rooms and stained glass windows from Tiffany's of New York. The mansion is open for tours May through October.

Continental Divide

P.O. Box 622
Ennis, MT 59729
(406) 682-7600

This always been one of the most often requested recipes at the Continental Divide. It's a great as an appetizer, luncheon entree or a midnight supper.

Tim Robbie, president of the Miami Dolphins, offered me four Super Bowl tickets for this recipe ! (Actually Tim got it for nothing because he's a great guy, plus he has super fishing on his ranch.)

C D Cajun Mushrooms
3   cups quartered mushrooms
1   cup crab meat
1/2 cup chopped sweet red peppers
1/2 cup chopped green onions
3 T butter
1 T thyme
1 T granulated garlic
1 T worcestershire
1 T Tabasco
    Salt to taste
3 cups whipping cream
2 T chopped fresh parsley

In a hot saute pan add 1 T butter and cook the mushrooms. Set aside in a baking dish. Melt the rest of the butter and add the peppers, onions, thyme and garlic. Saute until slightly cooked and add the rest of the ingredients. Cook for about 7 mins. on high heat until the cream is partially reduced. Salt to taste. Pour the mixture over the mushrooms and place in a hot oven until the cream mixture begins to thicken and bubble.

Sprinkle the chopped parsley over the top and serve with crunchy french or cuban bread to dip in the mixture. Serve with a crisp Sauvignon Blanc or very cold dry Champagne.

Jay and Karen Bentley

Jay and Karen Bentley treat visitors and Ennis locals to outstanding gourmet fare at the Continental Divide. Personal service and desserts to-die-for are just a small part of the wonderful experience that awaits you.

COPPER KING MANSION and GALLERY

This recipe was handed down by my great-grandmother who came to Butte from Montreal, Canada. It was a favorite of hers, a favorite of my mother's, and I often serve it in our restaurant at the Copper King Mansion.

FRENCH ONION SOUP

1-1/2 lbs. (5 cups) thinly
  sliced yellow onions
3 Tbls. butter
1 tsp. sugar
3 Tbls. flour
2 Quarts boiling brown
  (beef) stock or
  bouillon

1 Tbls. oil
1 tsp. salt
1/2 C. dry white wine
3 Tbls. cognac
1-1/2 C. grated
  parmesan cheese
Rounds of hard,
  toasted french
  bread

Cook the onions slowly with the butter and oil in a covered pan for 15 minutes. Uncover, raise heat to moderate and stir in the salt and sugar. Cook for 30-40 minutes stirring often, until the onions have turned a deep golden brown. Sprinkle in the flour and stir for 3 minutes. Remove from heat and blend in the boiling liquid. Add the wine and season to taste. Simmer, partially covered, for 30-40 minutes, skimming occasionally.

Just before serving, stir in the cognac. Pour into a soup tureen or soup bowls over the rounds of bread and pass the cheese separately.

For the toast rounds take 12-16 slices of French bread cut 1" thick. Place in a roasing pan (one layer deep) and bake in a 325-degree oven for 1/2 hour or until brown and dried out. Halfway through the baking, baste each side with a teaspoon of olive oil. Spread each side with grated parmesan cheese and brown under broiler.

Bon appetit!

Ann Cote' Sinttle

The Copper King Mansion in Butte was the home of William A. Clark. This 30-room Victorian mansion is a national historic site and guided tours are available throughout the summer.

Cordingley
Great Falls

Spicy Baked Shrimp

½ c. olive oil
2 Tbs. bottled Cajun seasoning
2 Tbs. fresh lemon juice
2 Tbs. chopped fresh parsley
1 Tbs. honey
1 Tbs. light soy sauce
1 pinch cayenne pepper

Take 2 lbs. of uncooked *fresh* large shrimp. Shell and devein.

Combine first seven ingredients in a 9" x 13" Pyrex baking dish. Add shrimp to ingredients and toss to coat. Cover with Saran wrap and refrigerate at least one hour.

Preheat oven to 450°.

Bake shrimp 10 minutes 'til cooked through. Stir occasionally.

Garnish with lemon wedges and parsley.

Can be served as an appetizer, or over rice with salad and French bread.

Mary E. Cordingley   *Bill Cordingley*

William A. Cordingley was the publisher of the Great Falls Tribune *for many years. He has won many Montana State Golf Championships, and was a member of the Federal Reserve Board. His wife, Mary, is an artist who is active in numerous community affairs, and is a past president of the Montana State University Advisory Board.*

Coyote Roadhouse Chefs' Selections

Dear Friends and the Inter-Mountain Childrens' Home,

The Coyote Roadhouse is pleased to give you one of our favorite and most popular recipes. We have often been asked for this particular recipe by our customers but have never divulged it until now.

This is a famous Cajun recipe from a little village deep in the Bayou. We hope you enjoy it as much as we.

Chicken-Sausage Jambalaya

1 Six pound hen, cut for frying	1 Cup green bell pepper, chop.
1 Tablespoon salt	3 Lrg. garlic cloves, minced
½ Tablespoon black pepper	2 Pounds smoked sausage, cut
1 Teaspoon dried thyme leaves	into 1 inch lengths
½ Tablespoon red pepper	3 Quarts water
½ Teaspoon rubbed sage	1 Bunch green onions, chopped
1 Cup oil	½ Bunch parsley, chopped
1 Large onion, minced	3/4 Cup canned tomato sauce
1 Cup celery, chopped	1 Cup peeled and chopped
	tomatoes
	6 Cups uncooked rice
	(converted)

1) Season chicken with salt and pepper.
2) In a large black iron pot, brown chicken in oil.
3) Add onions and garlic, cook until onions are clear.
4) Remove chicken, onions and garlic from pot.
5) Add sausage to oil and brown quickly.
6) Remove sausage and excess oil from pot.
7) Add chicken, onions, garlic, sausage and water to pot; cover pot and cook until chicken is tender, skimming excess fat from water. (be sure there are at least 11 cups of chicken stock in the pot. Chicken may be de-boned at this point and cut into small pieces.)
8) Add onion, green pepper, celery, green onions, tomatoes and tomato sauce, spices and rice; bring to a boil, stir and taste for seasonings.
9) Bake in 375 degree oven, covered, 45 min. or until rice is cooked and stock absorbed.

Enjoy!

Gary R. Hastings, Exec. Chef and Owner

Gary Hastings is the owner and chef of this country-style roadhouse in Bigfork. He is a master at cooking Cajun and Yucatan-style Mexican food. A multi-page menu complicates decision-making.

Stay Away, Joe Publishers
1500 Fourth Ave., North
Great Falls, Montana 59401

Fancy Six-Shooter Steak

2 full-cut round steaks, thick
1 t. peppercorns
1 c. flour
3 T. Worcestershire sauce
1 c. lard
Salt

Few range cooks had anything as fancy as Worcestershire sauce, in those days generally referred to just as Lea & Perrins. Cooks with the freight outfits which stopped at the army posts and towns along the road were able to keep better supplied. Worcestershire not only added flavor but served as a tenderizer because of the vinegar it contained.

To prepare a good six-shooter steak start by pulverizing the peppercorns. Don't grind them, just crush them on a slab of hardwood. Brush them into the cup of flour, any fragments left will be picked up when the steak is pounded. Cut the round steaks into the desired sizes. Do not trim off the fat. Using the butt of a six-shooter pound them while sprinkling them lightly with flour and pepper. Don't hammer. Merely lift the gun and let it fall. Its weight—2½ pounds loaded—will be sufficient. And don't work them down too thin. They are best reduced to about ⅔ of their original thickness. When each is finished sprinkle it with Worcestershire sauce. Stack the steaks one on the other and allow them to cure for half an hour. Melt lard in a covered skillet or Dutch oven and fry until browned while still raw in the middle. Salt, cover tightly and set off the heat. By the time the skillet is cool the steaks will be done all the way through and a gravy will be formed which delicately coats each of them.

From *Dan Cushman's Cow Country Cookbook,* by Dan Cushman

I began my writing career right near the top, as a newspaper correspondent. My territory was a good one; I was paid 15¢ an inch, headline deleted, by the Great Falls Tribune for all I could get printed; and my territory, Big Sandy, and the northern half of Chouteau County, was better than it may sound; Big Sandy then being, on good years, the largest cattle shipping point in the nation. On many months I'd realize $50 per month; clerks raked in $100 but they worked without glory.

DAN CUSHMAN

Dan Cushman was a reporter in Big Sandy for the Great Falls Tribune. *Among more than a dozen other novels, he wrote the memorable* Stay Away, Joe, *and also published* Dan Cushman's Cow Country Cookbook. *Dan lives in Great Falls.*

Corporate Office: Davidson Bldg., 8 Third St. No. • P.O. Box 5015
Great Falls, Montana 59403 • (406) 727-4200 • 1-800-332-5915

TENDERLOIN FILET WITH MUSHROOM WINE SAUCE

1 Whole Beef Tenderloin (apprx. 2½-3#). Remove fat and rub with butter. Bake @ 400°, 20 mts. (Have tenderloin at room temp. before baking.) Cover with Marinade and bake 20 mts. longer. Let stand 10 mts. after removing from oven. Slice into 1/2" slices and serve with Wine Mushroom Sauce. Serves 4-6.

MARINADE
(For 2 Tenderloins)

1/4 C	Chopped Onion	Saute onion in butter in small skillet. Then
2 T	Butter	add other ingredients. You can cover tender-
2 T	Soy Sauce	loins with this Marinade early in the day and
1 t	Dijon Mustard	leave in refrigerator--or cover during baking.
3/4 C	Sherry	

WINE MUSHROOM SAUCE

6 T	Butter or Margarine		2 T	Worchestershire Sauce
2 Med.	Chopped Onions			Pinch of Thyme
1 3/4#	Thin Sliced Mushrooms		5 oz.	Dry Red Wine
2 T	Catsup		1	Bullion Beef Cube,
3 T	Flour			Dissolved in 1/4 C Water.

In large skillet, saute onion in butter. Add other ingredients, except mushrooms. Stir constantly until heated through and blended. (Can be made earlier and reheated just before serving.) Add mushrooms after heated and stir gently. Serve with tenderloin.

One of Montana's many pleasures is its homegrown beef--which also contributes to the pleasure of serving this delightful entree--a special treat--it's #1 on our hit parade. ENJOY!

Ian B. Davidson
Chairman and
Chief Executive Officer

Sour Cream
Beef and Bean Enchiladas

1 1/2 Pounds of ground beef
1 medium onion, chopped
1 #1 can of refried beans
1 tsp. salt
1/2 tsp. garlic powder
1/3 cup taco sauce
1 cup sliced olives (pitted)
2 cans (10 oz.) enchilada sauce
12 corn tortillas
3 cups shredded cheddar cheese (10 oz.)

Saute beef and onions until meat is brown. Drain excess
fat. Stir in beans, salt, garlic and taco sauce. Heat until
bubbly.

Heat enchilada sauce. Pour 1 can into an ungreased, shallow
3 quart baking dish. Pour about 1/4 " of oil in a medium frying
pan and heat. Dip tortillas 1 at a time in the hot oil to soften
and put on paper towels to drain quickly.

Place about 1/3 cup ground beef filling in each tortilla and
roll to close. Place seam down in sauce in baking dish. Top
with remaining can of enchilada sauce and cover with cheese.

Bake uncovered for about 15 minutes at 350 degrees. It may
be covered and refrigerated for a day or frozen. If taken directly from refrigerator - increase baking time to 45 minutes.
If frozen bake for 1 hour and 15 minutes at 325 degrees.

Garnish with olive slices and sour cream.
Serves 6-8 people.

This is a real family favorite of ours. I always triple
this recipe and freeze two of them for another time. I also
sometimes increase the refried beans and omit the meat for vege-
tarian enchiladas.

This is one of many recipes which we have tasted first and
collected in our many years of traveling with Athletes in Action,
and with World and Olympic wrestling teams.

Gene Davis

Gene Davis is a four-time state wrestling champion from Missoula County High School. He won four national freestyle
championships and a bronze medal in the 1976 Montreal Olympics. He coached the U.S. team in the 1988 Olympics
in Seoul, South Korea.

SAN FRANCISCO 49ERS

Edward J. DeBartolo, Jr.
Owner/Chairman of the Board

MARINARA SAUCE

Ingredients

1   12 oz. can tomato paste
4   28 oz. cans whole tomatoes (run through blender)
4   cloves garlic, chopped
1   medium onion, chopped
4   tablespoons oil
1   pound pasta, any kind
    handful parsley
2   tablespoons sugar

- In a 6-quart pot, sauté chopped garlic in oil
- Add chopped onion and cook until soft and transparent
- Add whole tomatoes that have been put through the blender
- Add the tomato paste and stir until mixed well
- Add the sugar and parsley and cook slowly for approximately 1 1/2 hours, stirring occasionally
- Spoon over pasta and serve immediately

COOKING TIPS - For a spicier flavor add one teaspoon of crushed red pepper while sauce is simmering

EDWARD J. DeBARTOLO, JR.

Edward J. DeBartolo, Jr., owner of the National Football League San Francisco 49ers, is active in many charities. His Montana ranch is near Whitefish.

This recipe was developed by our executive chef, Steve Goodman, in response to our customers's requests for more chicken dishes. The quality of the chicken is important, but the richness of the sauce is what really defines this dinner. Hope you enjoy it.

Ed Wells

Ed Wells

CHICKEN WITH SUN DRIED TOMATOES

2 6 OZ CHICKEN BREASTS, SKIN REMOVED
3 TBSP OLIVE OIL
½ CUP COARSELY CHOPPED SUN DRIED TOMATOES, RECONSTITUTED
1/8 CUP DRY SHERRY
½ CUP CHICKEN STOCK
¼ CUP HEAVY WHIPPING CREAM
3 TBSP CHOPPED GREEN ONION, MOSTLY GREEN TOPS
SALT AND PEPPER

OVER MEDIUM HIGH HEAT, BROWN CHICKEN IN OLIVE OIL. TURN OVER, ADD TOMATOES, SHAKING PAN BRIEFLY WHILE COOKING ON MEDIUM HIGH FOR 2 MINUTES MORE. REDUCE HEAT TO MEDIUM. DEGLAZE PAN WITH SHERRY AND ADD CHICKEN STOCK. ADD CREAM AND COOK 3 MINUTES REDUCING THE SAUCE. REDUCE HEAT TO LOW AND SIMMER UNTIL DONE. TOSS IN ONIONS AND CHECK THE SEASONING. SERVE.

The Depot was established in 1974 near Missoula's old railroad station. It is well known for prime rib, steak, seafood and chicken dishes. A local favorite place to eat where the food is always great.

Dirty Shame Saloon

Dick McGary, Owner   29453 Yaak River Road   (406) 295-5439
                            Troy, Montana 59935

I came up with this way of cooking grouse as I was tired of the traditional Mountain Man style grouse dipped in seasoned flour and fried in grease. This is just one of several ways that I use different seasonings to enhance the unique flavor of grouse. Hope you enjoy it as much as I do!

Different kinds of foul may be substituted to this recipe providing a variety of flavors unique to each species.

Dick McGary

ALMOND GROUSE STRIPS

3 grouse breasts
1 cup white flour
½ c. finely ground almonds
2 Tbsp. chervil

½ tsp. white pepper
salt to taste
3 eggs, beaten
½ tsp. onion powder

Slice grouse breast ¼ to ½ inch strips and blot dry. Blend flour and ground almonds together with 1½ Tbsp. chervil, pepper and salt. Coat grouse strips with flour mixture and set aside. Add rest of chervil, onion powder, and salt and pepper to taste to the beaten eggs. Dip grouse strips in egg mixture and into flour and shake well until flour is absorbed. Repeat dipping, if necessary to build up coating. Saute strips in hot butter for 1½ minutes or until lightly browned. Serve with horseradish, ketchup, or a spicy mustard dip.

The Dirty Shame Saloon, located in the far northwest corner of Montana, has a history as rugged and wild as the wilderness that surrounds it. Nestled in the Yaak Valley, the Dirty Shame is in one of America's last outbacks. A sign over the bar door warning "Please check your guns at the bar" says it all.

MONTE DOLACK GRAPHICS

BLACK BEAN SALMON BAR-B-Q

Ingredients:
        One whole salmon or two large salmon fillets
        1 tsp. Fermented black beans (dried)
        6 ozs. beer (your choice)
        1 tsp. sugar
        ¼ cup soy sauce
        ¼ cup sesame oil
        Cilantro-a few pinches
        Tin foil
        Bar-b-que grill and charcoal (I use a Weber brand with cover)

Rinse a cleaned salmon throughly (or use 2 large salmon fillets)
Fillet a salmon into 2 large steaks.
Form a double tin foil "boat" for each fillet approximately the same
size as each fillet with 1 inch walls to hold in juices.

The marinade:
Finely chop fermented black beans, stir in 6 ozs. of the beer, drink the
rest. Add sugar, and soy sauce. Mix throughly and pour over each fillet.
Let stand for 15 minutes.

Grill over hot coals for approximately 15 minutes or until done. Remove
from grill. Place fillets on a platter.

Pour crackling hot sesame oil over each fillet and sprinkle with
cilantro.

Serve while hot-it is delicious!

I like to serve this salmon dish with a fresh green salad, baked potato,
and fresh steamed asparagus. A fine white wine and of course good
music!

MONTE DOLACK

Monte Dolack grew up in Great Falls and studied at the University of Montana under Rudy Autio and Robert DeWeese.
He opened his graphic design studio in 1974. He is currently building a large portfolio of hand-made, original
lithographs. Monte and his artist wife, Mary Beth Percival, live in Missoula.

BLACK-EYED PEA DIP

In Texas, it is a custom to eat black-eyed peas on New Year's Day for good luck through the coming year. I served this Black-Eyed Pea Dip on many a New Year's Day when the Cowboys needed all the luck they could get. Sometimes it worked, sometimes … Well, it tastes great <u>any</u> time of the year.

The Tex-Mex heritage of Texas is evident in this recipe. I would suggest adjusting the number of jalepenos to suit your tolerance for hot food. As written, the recipe is *definitely* for experienced taste buds.

DICE:

1/2 bell pepper	2 stalks celery
8 jalepeno peppers	1 large onion

ADD:

1 tsp coarse black pepper	2 tsp Tabasco
1/2 cup Ketchup	3 chicken bouillon cubes

BRING TO SIMMER. Then ADD:

1 tsp salt	3 cans black-eyed peas
1 can tomatoes	1 tsp garlic powder

COOK 30 MINUTES. Then BLEND:
3 tbsp flour & 1/2 cup bacon grease; combine to thicken.

Serve heated in a bowl with tortilla chips on side.

Pat Donovan

Pat Donovan was raised in Helena. He was an All-American football player at Stanford University and played offensive lineman for the Dallas Cowboys from 1975 to 1983. In those years, the team won the NFC Championship three times, and the Super Bowl once. Pat lives in Dallas and has a home in Whitefish.

— **54** —

P.O. Box 747 • Seeley Lake, Montana 59868 • (406) 677-2777

Wherever I've lived, from St. Thomas to Seattle, one of my greatest interests has been developing original recipes from local products. Having a special affection for my native state, I'm pleased to share this "Made in Montana" recipe.

MONTANA TROUT ROLLED WITH SMOKED SALMON AND WATERCRESS
SERVED WITH ROASTED RED PEPPER BUTTER

Trout

Yield: 2 servings

Ingredients:
2 6 oz. trout fillets
2 oz. thinly sliced smoked salmon
2 oz. blanched watercress
pinch of salt
freshly cracked white pepper

Method of Preparation:
1. Skin, trim and bone the fillets
2. Slightly flatten fillets by placing under plastic wrap and slapping with a mallet
3. Place each fillet skin side up on a 12" x 12" piece of cheesecloth and season with salt and pepper
4. Lay the smoked salmon on the trout and follow with the blanched watercress
5. Roll each fillet into a tight pinwheel and poach in court bouillon for 10 to 12 minutes
6. When ready to serve, remove the cheesecloth and slice into 1 inch wheels
7. Serve with Roasted Red Pepper Butter

Roasted Red Pepper Butter

Yield: 10 oz.

Ingredients:
8 oz. unsalted butter
1 red pepper
1 T. minced green herbs
1 T. chopped parsley
1 T. fresh lemon juice
1 tsp. grated orange zest
salt and pepper

Method of Preparation:
1. Roast whole red pepper over open flame until pepper is completely black
2. Cool under cold running water. Remove blackened skin and rinse out seeds
3. Finely chop roasted pepper
4. In a food processor, whip the butter until light and creamy. Slowly add lemon juice, chopped red pepper, herbs, orange zest and salt and pepper
5. Place on plastic wrap and roll into a cylinder. Hold in refrigerator until needed
6. When ready to serve, slice medallions of red pepper butter, place on trout pinwheels and heat in oven for one minute

The Double Arrow Lodge located in the Swan Valley has exceptional food, gracious service and beautiful surroundings. Chef Doug Day, a Montana native, uses local products incorporated with his classical French training to please diners.

Pork Roast with Plum Sauce   serves 6-8

EAGLE BEND
GOLFING COMMUNITY

P.O. Box 960

Bigfork, Montana 59911

1-800-255-5641

(406) 837-5641 Fax (406) 837-3851

3 - 3½ pound boneless pork roast
    salt

Plum Sauce
    2 cups catsup
    2/3 cup sugar
    2 tablespoons hoisin sauce
    2 teaspoons sesame oil
    ½ tablespoon fresh ginger, minced
    ½ tablespoon salt
    2 teaspoons liquid smoke
    2 cloves garlic, minced
    1/3 cup vinegar

Salt the pork roast and brown in a dutch oven. Cover and simmer
for 1 hour. Pour off fat. Combine sauce ingredients. Add half
the plum sauce to pork and continue cooking for 1½ hours. Turn
roast periodically. Heat and serve the remaining sauce with the
pork.

This sauce works well with chicken and pork ribs.

This is a family favorite that we found in a restaurant in Maui,
Hawaii years ago.

Enjoy!
Patty and Mike Felt

---

*Eagle Bend Golf Course was named by Golf Digest as one of the top 50 public courses in America and also as the
number-two new public golf course in America in 1989.*

BARBECUE PORK TENDERLOIN

TRIM THE FAT FROM A PORK TENDERLOIN (OR TWO) AND MARINATE

FOR FOUR HOURS. COOK ON LOW HEAT ON BARBECUE FOR 50-60

MINUTES, TURNING EVERY TEN MINUTES AND BRUSHING WITH MARINADE

EACH TIME. SLICE AND SERVE WITH NEW POTATOES, FRESH GREEN

SALAD AND SOURDOUGH BREAD. A PINOT NOIR GOES WELL WITH

WITH THIS COMBINATION.

MARINADE:

    1 PART DRY VERMOUTH
    1 PART DARK MOLASSES
    1 PART LOW SALT SOY SAUCE

BE CERTAIN TO COOK PORK WELL. I HAVE USED THIS MENU YEAR

ROUND, BUT THE FAMILY PARTICULARLY LIKES IT IN THE SUMMER

FOR A RELAXING EVENING ON THE PATIO.

DR. BRUCE CARPENTER

Eastern Montana College in Billings was established March 12, 1927, to train elementary school teachers. It is now a comprehensive multi-purpose state college with programs in the arts and sciences, teacher preparation, business and economics, human services and some professional areas. It is the major education center in eastern Montana.

WILDERNESS OUTFITTERS

Smoke and Thelma Elser
Telephone (406) 549-2820
3800 Rattlesnake Drive
Missoula, Montana 59802

While traveling, via pack string, in the high country of the Bob Marshall Wilderness I have been confronted many times with the responsibility for preparing a quick and substantial meal for my guests. Salad, vegetable, meat and potatoes are the normal fare in my camp. Because I often camp in high alpine meadows and cook over a collapsible wood stove many of my meals consist of a fried main dish. Making casseroles and boiling potatoes at high altitudes is slow and difficult. I heard of an old sheep herder recipe to cook potatoes, making them easier and quicker to cook in the high country without frying. Below is the way I prepare sheep herder potatoes and I have found that my guests enjoy the change.

SHEEP HERDER POTATOES

In a deep 10-12" camp skillet (preferably cast iron) brown 10 thick slices of bacon. Drain off at least half the bacon grease and remove the bacon. Thoroughly wash 6 - 8 medium potatoes (peeled or unpeeled). Chunk potatoes and 1 medium onion in 1/2" pieces. Add 3 cups hot water and bring to a boil. Boil about 10 minutes or until potatoes are somewhat tender but still solid. Be sure that about 1" of water remains. Add 1 can evaporated milk and 1/2 can water. Crumble the bacon into the skillet and bring back to a simmer. Simmer until sauce reaches a desirable thickness. Add salt and pepper to taste. Can be served with 3-4 slices of cheddar cheese on top.

Bring a hardy appetite and enjoy watching the sun set over our beautiful Rocky Mountains and hearing the horse bells ringing in the meadow. Appreciate the flavor of good Montana beef and my famous sheep herder potatoes as you eat a meal that will get you over the ridge and through the next day.

Oh yes, be sure to properly dispose of your bacon grease. In the back country I burn it in a good hot fire in the stove or pack it out in a well sealed, odor proof container. Otherwise you might attract some unwanted dinner guests!

Smoke

Since 1957 Smoke Elser has been a professional outfitter and guide. He is a leader in the promotion of minimum impact camping, giving many seminars on the subject each year. He is the author of Packin' in on Mules and Horses.

Camarones al ajillo

1½lbs large shrimp- peeled and butterflied
¼lbs. butter
½ cup dry white wine
4 large cloves garlic- put through garlic press
½ cup chopped parsley
½ cup chopped cilantro

Melt butter on low heat in large skillet. Add pressed garlic and saute for about 3 minutes, stirring constantly- make certain that the butter or garlic does not burn. Add wine, half of parsley, and half of cilantro. Bring to a boil to evaporate alcohol. Add the shrimp and the rest of the greens and cook for about 1 minute- be careful not to over cook shrimp.

Serve with chilled white dry wine and crisp French bread to soak up the juices!

Buen provecho!!!

TYPED BY PABLITO ELVIRA (PABLO ELVIRA'S SON)

Pablo Elvira is a leading baritone for the New York Metropolitan Opera. He is the main force behind Bozeman's Rocky Mountain Opera Company, and owns a home near Bozeman.

"Bringing Home the Bacon"

"Bringing Home the Bacon", an original sketch by Fred Fellows.

COWMAN'S SPAGHETTI

Wipe off	2 lb. CHUCK ROAST
Dredge roast in	$\frac{1}{4}$ C. FLOUR
	1 Tsp. SALT
	$\frac{1}{2}$ Tsp. PEPPER
Heat in skillet or dutch oven	2 Tbsp. WESSON OIL

Brown roast on both sides in hot oil.
When roast is brown, pour off excess
fat.   Add the following ingredients
and simmer about 3 hours.............

14$\frac{1}{2}$ Oz. can TOMATOES
1 can TOMATOE PASTE
1 can TOMATOE SAUCE
1 small clove GARLIC
1$\frac{1}{2}$ Tsp. SALT
1 BAY LEAF

30 minutes before sauce id done add.. $\frac{1}{4}$ Tsp. OREGANO

Remove the roast and bay leaf and serve
the sauce over buttered spaghetti. You
may cool the roast and slice it to eat
with the spaghetti or you can use it
for sandwiches.

This is a "he-man recipe" that can be used with an ELK ROAST
as well as beef.

Fred Fellows

---

*Fred Fellows is an award-winning western artist, and past president and current director of the world-famous Cowboy
Artists of America. He was selected by the Hesston Corporation to do a series of paintings, sculptures and belt buckles for
the National Finals Rodeo each year. Fred and his wife, Deborah, live in Woods Bay on Flathead Lake.*

This recipe was made for the adventure-some cook. This creation came about with a little ingenuity, a lot of different ingredients and no cook for Steakfry Day. It's a little bit of this, a lot of that and is made according to the cook's taste. Note: This is the most requested recipe at the Ranch.

MAUREEN'S BAKED BEANS

Molasses	Pork N Beans
Brown Sugar	Honey
Ketchup	Worcestershire Sauce
Soy Sauce	Very Well Done Bacon, Chopped
Finely, Diced Onions	

SPICES - Red spices, just a dash -- Green spices, in equal amounts and White spices, in small amounts. Remember it is according to your tastes.

Tarragon	Marjoram
Basil	Thyme
Rosemary	Oregano
Cayenne	Chili Powder
Paprika	Onion Powder
Garlic	Ground Mustard

Mix all ingredients together, sauce should be a rich mahogney color with a sweet, zippy taste. Bake at 200 degrees for 4 to 5 hours. Best beans you will ever taste!

Chocolate-lovers paradise, this Brownie recipe is one of a kind, gooey on the inside and soft on the outside. This is the second most requested recipe.

UNDONE BROWNIES

1 Cup Margarine	2 Cups Sugar
4 Eggs	1 1/3 Cups Flour
2 Tsp. Vanilla	4 Melted, Unsweetened Choc. Squares

Combine all the ingredients and mix well; pour into a greased 9 x 13 pan and bake at 325 degrees for 20 to 25 minutes. They are done when the Brownies pull away from the edges of the pan.

Maureen Averill

Flathead Lake Lodge • Box 248 • Bigfork, Montana 59911 • (406) 837-4391

DAN AVERILL
SECRETARY-TREASURER
DARV AVERILL
VICE PRESIDENT

LES AVERILL
PRESIDENT

DOUG AVERILL
DIRECTOR
DALVIN AVERILL
DIRECTOR

Flathead Lake Lodge
Quarter Circle LA Dude Ranch
PHONE 837-4391 — AREA CODE 406
Bigfork, Montana
59911

It's Happy Hour time at the Ranch.
The most popular of all the hors d' oeuvres is our
Mexican Party Dip

1 lb. Kraft American Cheese - cubed
1 small onion minced
2 Jalopeno chile pepper's - rinced, seeded & minced
1 16 oz. can chili with no beans

Mix in casserole dish, bake @ 350 degrees for one hour, stir occasionally.
Will serve a party of 20. Double the recipe for large groups.
Serve hot with tortilla chips.

This was given to us by one of our lodge guests.

Les & Ginny Averill

In 1945, Les Averill had a dream to build a family style dude ranch on the shores of Flathead Lake. Today this ranch is one of the premier vacation spots in America. Activities, food and personal service are of the highest quality and keep guests returning year after year. The lodge is now operated by Les's son Doug and his wife, Maureen.

BLACK BEAN SOUP

        2 cups dry black beans
        8 cups water or stock

Soak beans overnight. Rinse beans and put in heavy soup pot with
8 cups water or stock. Bring to a boil, lower heat and simmer
slowly for 2 hours. Then add:

        2 onions, chopped
        3 cloves garlic
        2 large carrots, chopped
        1 tsp. ground coriander
        1 1/2 tsp. ground cumin

Add all above ingredients to soup pot. Simmer for 30 minutes or
until carrots are tender. Then add:

        2 oranges, peeled, sectioned and seeded
        1/2 cup orange juice
        1 Tbs. dry sherry
        1/4 tsp. black pepper
        1/2 tsp. lemon juice
        1/4 tsp. cayenne

Add all ingredients to soup pot. Simmer for about 15 minutes.
Turn heat off and cool slightly. Process until smooth. Return to
pot and heat before serving. Serve with a dollop of nonfat yogurt.
Serves 6.   Calories - 80 per serving.   Fat - 1.4 gm per serving.

Jane Fonda   Ted Turner

*Jane Fonda is twice an Academy Award winner, an activist and author of exercise books and video tapes.
Ted Turner is president and CEO of Turner Broadcasting Systems, Inc. and CNN. He owns the Atlanta Braves and the
Atlanta Hawks. He and Jane own a large ranch by Gallatin Gateway and another ranch near Helena.*

PETER FONDA

ANTELOPE BOLOGNESE SAUCE

In a large sauce pan heat 1 tablespoon olive oil
Add one finely chopped large sweet onion. Stir
and cook until transparent, remove from pan.
Add 2 pounds ground antelope and brown over
medium heat, stir to separate, then add 2 large
cans of Italian tomatoes, ½ cup of GOOD CA. red
wine, 2 tablespoons sugar, season with a lot of
basil, fresh if you can, 1 tab. oregano, salt and
pepper to taste, 3 large cloves fresh minced garlic,
don't cook the garlic with onions, makes it taste
bitter. Simmer several hours, stirring frequently.
This is not a thin sauce. Serve with Linguine
and lots of fresh grated parmesan cheese.
As the people at your table consume this meal you
will notice they start with an accent and end
speaking fluent Italian.
This is especially wonderful when my wife cooks
and I don't...
Yes, I typed this whole thing, AFTER I made the
sauce.

Peter Fonda is an actor, director, writer and producer. He and his wife, Becky, own a ranch in the Paradise Valley south of Livingston. He is best known for his starring role in the classic Easy Rider. He is the son of Henry Fonda and brother of Jane Fonda.

Todd "Kid" Foster

Knockout Hamburger Soup

1 lb. hamburger or turkey burger
1 medium can of tomato paste
1 medium can of tomato sauce
2 potatoes (peeled & cubed) or 2 cans of sliced potatoes
4 carrots (peeled and sliced)
4 ribs of celery (sliced)
½ c. instant rice
4 beef bouillon cubes
dash of salt and pepper
6 c. boiling water

Brown burger and drain grease. In soup pot, add burger and remaining ingredients to boiling water. Let veggies cook medium to low for about 20 minutes.

Shake in some Worcestershire sauce and serve!

Currently [spring 1992], I'm 22-0 with 19 knockouts. I'm rated number ten in the world by the International Boxing Federation. I should be fighting for the World Lightweight Championship by the end of 1992. I'm hoping to fight for the title somewhere in Montana.

Todd Foster is a professional boxer from Great Falls, who competed in the 1988 Olympic Games and is rated number 10 in the world by the International Boxing Federation. He is a contender for the World Lightweight Boxing Championship.

Francis Real Estate

(406) 287-3263
Fax (406) 287-5763
1-800-735-8547

P.O. Box 492
Whitehall, MT 59759

KAHUNA'S TUNA SANDWICH

After playing a game, even the most infinitesimal task is a real effort, but this is almost as easy as ordering a pizza.

FILLING:

1 can tuna, drained   cheddar cheese
3 hard boiled eggs, chopped   tomato slices
3 green onions, chopped (3 T.)   Syrian pocket bread
3 T. sweet pickle relish
salt
mayonnaise

Combine ingredients for filling. Cut Syrian loaves in half width-wise and add filling, tomato slices and cheese. Heat on a cookie sheet in 350° oven approximately 15-20 minutes. Ideally the cheese should be just on the verge of oozing forth. To catch it at this moment is to catch it at its peak. It also saves having to scrub burnt cheese off the cookie sheet. Makes 6 sandwiches.

Russ Francis, Owner

In 1975, Russ Francis was a first-round draft pick of the New England Patriots. An all-pro tight end, he played for the San Francisco 49ers in 1982 and was a member of the 1985 Super Bowl Championship team. He retired in 1989 and came to Montana. He owns a real estate business in Whitehall with property there and in the Bitterroot Valley.

Gamers
Fine Confectionery

Gamer's Confectionery, Inc.

15 West Park Street
Butte, Montana

Carl Rowan, Proprietor

painting by Elizabeth Lochrie

Gamers Confectionery, Montana

*Founded in 1905, this restaurant in Butte is one of the oldest
business concerns in the young state of Montana. A favorite with
Gamers' customers for half a century is Cornish pasties, an Old World
meat pie introduced to the area by early settlers — Cornish, Welsh, and Irish
miners. A retail shop for baked goods and candy is operated next to the
dining room at 15 West Park Street. Open 8:00 a.m. to 4:00 p.m.
for breakfast and lunch every weekday; closed on Sunday.*

Hot Cornish Pasty
1 pound sirloin tip
3 raw potatoes, cut fine
3 green onions, cut fine
Salt and pepper, to taste
    Cut steak in small cubes, add vegetables
and seasonings. Mix well.

Pastry
4 cups flour
1 cup lard
1 ounce butter
2 teaspoons salt
Pinch of baking powder

Cut shortenings into flour and add enough
cold water to make a stiff dough. Roll out about
1/8 inch thick and cut 6 circles about 6 inches in
diameter. A saucer is a good guide. Into the center
of each circle put a mound of filling ingredients.
Moisten around the edge of the pasty and press
halves together at the edges with a fork. Brush
each with a mixture of 1 egg and 1 tablespoon of
cream beaten together. Make a hole in each to let
steam escape. Bake at 425° for 1 hour. Serves 6.

*Only in Butte would you find good food, service with personality, and the insistence that you ring up, pay, and make
change on the bill, yourself. A meal here is a must!*

GIRDLE MOUNTAIN SUMMER HOUSE
Restaurant

A favorite entrée at Girdle Mountain Summer House is Cornish Game Hen with Gorgonzola & Port. Delicious as a dinner entrée, these hens are also wonderful for a picnic lunch. After a full week of restaurant related activities, we love to escape to the Monarch area and enjoy these tasty leftovers served with crusty bread, crudités, grapes and a crisp white wine. Then we follow lunch with a long nap in the sun to become rejuvenated and ready for the work deluge of the new week.

Enjoy!

Sherrill Halbe

Cornish Game Hen with Gorgonzola & Port

per person

1	Cornish game hen
1oz.	Gorgonzola cheese, 1/4" slice
1T	Butter, cut in pieces
1 clove	Garlic, sliced
1/4 c	White Port wine
	Salt & pepper

Cut hens in half and remove wing tips. Pat dry and season with salt & pepper. Carefully insert a slice of cheese between the skin and breast of each half. Place hen, breast side up, in a baking dish, dot with butter and garlic slices, then pour wine over all. Bake at 400° for about 45 minutes or until the meat juice runs clear when a leg is pierced. While baking, baste the hens every 10 minutes with pan juices.

The Girdle Mountain Summer House in Belt is like a charming French country inn. Owner Sherrill Halbe, a native of Great Falls, returns each June from her home in San Francisco to create outstanding gourmet meals that are served by reservation only.

United States Department of the Interior

NATIONAL PARK SERVICE
Glacier National Park
West Glacier, Montana 59936

IN REPLY REFER TO:

H. Gilbert Lusk
Superintendent

While in Big Bend, Texas, our fund raising activities included auctions. This cake was donated to be auctioned by a native Texan (who managed to keep the recipe secret for many years) and always sold for $35 or $40. The name of the cake is a clue to its richness!

Nieman-Marcus Cake

Mix until creamy --

  1 package dry cake mix -- we prefer a yellow cake with pudding in the mix

  2 eggs

  1 stick softened butter (1/2 cup)

Spread into 9" x 13" cake pan.

Mix together --

  1 box powdered sugar

  2 eggs

  1 8oz package of cream cheese, softened

Spread on top of cake mix.

Bake 30-35 minutes at 350 degrees.

NOTE: Don't be alarmed when cake falls in the middle. It's supposed to. This is very rich -- cut like bars instead of cake.

People eating this cake regularly are guaranteed not to fall in the middle
Happy eating
gil

Glacier National Park is one of the jewels of the national park system. It is located in northwest Montana along the Canada border and straddles the Continental Divide. Although there are 60 active glaciers in the park today, the name is derived from the intense glacial sculpting of the park's mountain country.

Glacier Raft Company

NO. 6 GOING-TO-THE-SUN ROAD
P.O. BOX 218 — WEST GLACIER, MT 59936
RESERVATIONS: 1-800-332-9995 — OFFICE: 406-888-5454 — FAX: 406-888-5541

BEST CAKE

Bake @ 350   30-35 min.

Put everything in one bowl and mix with wooden spoon.

    2 C. unsifted flour
    2 C. sugar
    2 eggs
    2 tsp. baking soda
    1 C. chopped walnuts
    1 #303 can or 16 oz. **undrained** crushed pineapple
    1 tsp. vanilla

Bake in 13x9x2 **ungreased pan.**

Ice with **Cream Cheese Icing**

    1 1/2 C. sifted confectioners sugar
    1 stick margarine
    8 oz. cream cheese
    1 tsp vanilla

A favorite birthday cake of our guides! My Mom said — try this — everyone will say it's just the "Best Cake" — and it is — easy too!

Sally Thompson

Gourmet Girls at Large
Catering & Party Planning

Trudy Waldo
406-446-1095
Sylvia Adams
406-446-1868

P.O. Box 814
Red Lodge, MT 59068

Dear Friends of the Intermountain Children's Home:

During the time that we operated our restaurant, Sylvia's Good Food in Red Lodge, Montana, we concocted this zesty chicken wing appetizer -- it was one of the most popular items on the menu. The recipe was published in the August, 1987 monthly Bon Appetit Magazine at the request of a patron, and later published in the Cooking With Bon Appetit Recipe Yearbook 1988.

LOUISIANA HOT CHICKEN WINGS

6 to 8 servings

1/2 # butter
1 teaspoon garlic powder
8 tablespoons hot pepper sauce
1/2 cup fresh lemon juice
1 teaspoon dried red pepper flakes
2 teaspoons dried oregano
1 teaspoon dried basil
1/2 teaspoon dried marjoram
1/2 teaspoon dried rosemary
1/2 teaspoon dried thyme

24 chicken wings, cut in half at joint

Melt butter in heavy medium saucepan. Add remaining ingredients except chicken and simmer 1 hour, stirring occasionally.

Preheat oven to 400 degrees F. Arrange chicken wings on shallow baking sheet. Bake wings until lightly browned -- about 30 minutes. Drain chicken fat. Brush wings generously with sauce. Continue baking until very crisp, 15 to 20 minutes. Reheat sauce. Serve chicken wings immediately. Pass remaining sauce separately.

Sylvia Adams and Trudy Waldo of Red Lodge specialize in catering gourmet fare that is as tasty as it is fresh and original. They have done catering for several Hollywood stars and for movies being filmed in Montana.

DONNA GRADY'S GISHY-GOOEY COOKIES

When I was growing up in Shelby, my mother made baking into an art form. When I left home and became a bachelor writer, I yearned for her deserts, and while most of them were beyond my primitive culinary skills, the following recipe was something even I could handle. The result redefines the genre of *chocolate cookies*.

Ingredients (for a double batch):

4 cups sugar
1 cup butter (2 cubes)
1 cup milk
2 tsp vanilla
6 cups oatmeal
1/2 cup Hershey's cocoa

Optional ingredients:
1 1/2 cup coconut
1 cup chopped walnuts

* Mix all dry ingredients except sugar in a large bowl.
* In saucepan, heat sugar, butter, milk and vanilla. When they boil, continue boil for ONE minute, then pour into bowl of dry ingredients. Mix thoroughly.
* Drop onto cookie sheets in desired size (small is sufficient), let cool.

James Grady

James Grady is from Shelby. His first novel, Six Days of the Condor, *was made into a Hollywood movie,* Three Days of the Condor. *He has written many novels since then, including his latest spy-thriller,* River of Darkness.

GRANDSTREET THEATRE

Ambrosia

Two weeks before an opening night, the cast and crew of that particular
show celebrate set-in day with a potluck. Special friends are remembered
as we share recipes. Thanks to our friend, Lex Wadsworth, from Scapinol,
Spokane Civic Theatre.

1/2	cup chopped onion
1/2	cup butter
1	cup beef boullion broth
1	tablespoon cornstarch
1/2	teaspoon majoram
1 1/2	pounds fresh mushrooms
1/2	tablespoon dry sherry
2	tablespoons snipped parsley
1/2	cup crumbled crackers
2	tablespoons parmesan cheese with 1 tablespoon butter

Saute mushrooms and onions in butter. Blend boullion with cornstarch and
majoram. Add to mushrooms and onions. Stir until mixture thickens.
Remove from heat. Add wine and parsley. Pour into one quart casserole
dish. Combine crumbs, parmesan cheese and butter. Sprinkle on top. Bake
at 350 degrees for 20 minutes or until hot and bubbly.

Don & Janet McLaughlin

P.O. Box 1258
Helena, Mt. 59624

Box Office: 443-3311
Business Office: 442-4270

*Grand Street Theatre is Helena's year-round, self-supporting community theater bringing local stagehands, directors,
amateur performers and an occasional professional onto the boards to "strut their stuff" in everything from the classics to
contemporary comedy. It is housed in an historical building dating from 1901, which features an original Tiffany window.*

Italian Chicken

Ingredients:

One Roasting Chicken
One Fresh Lemon
Olive Oil
Italian Seasoning

Wash chicken thoroughly and place in baking dish.

Rub two to three tablespoons of olive oil on chicken and add a little to bottom of baking dish.

Squeeze the juice of the lemon over entire chicken and on the inside.

Sprinkle Italian Seasonings all over chicken - top and bottom.

Cook at 375' for approximately one hour.
Longer for large chicken and less if only doing chicken breasts.

Serve with new red potatoes - baked, fresh garden salad and freshly baked bread.

My wife, Leesa and I like to entertain on the spur of the moment and spontaneously invite people to our home. Leesa created this recipe one night and all of our guests raved! Since, we have used this recipe repeatedly for family and friends when we want to serve something fun and tasty!

We hope all who try this simple recipe will enjoy it!

Best Wishes,

Ray Klesh
General Manager

The Great Falls Dodgers joined the Pioneer League in 1948, as the Selectrics, a locally owned team. In the late 1950s they became the Electrics and, in 1969, the Giants, finally affiliating with the L.A. Dodgers in 1983. They are in the advanced rookie classification of the National Association of Professional Baseball.

STOUFFER WAVERLY HOTEL
2450 Galleria Parkway • Atlanta, Georgia 30339
(404) 953-4500 • FAX: (404) 951-1321

Joseph D. Guilbault
Senior Vice President/General Manager

These may be called "Nantucket" Morning Glory Muffins, but I can assure you they go just fine with morning coffee in Big Sky country! My wife, Lucy, and I enjoy them regularly when we spend our summers at our home in Kalispell...sipping coffee on the deck as we watch the sunrise on Flathead Lake! Hope you enjoy them as much as we do.

Joe & Lucy Guilbault

NANTUCKET MORNING GLORY MUFFINS

4 cups all purpose flour
2½ cups sugar
4 tsp. soda
4 tsp. cinnamon
1 tsp. salt
4 cups peeled, grated apples
1 cup raisins

1 cup chopped pecans
1 cup shredded coconut
1 cup grated carrot
6 eggs
2 cups vegetable oil
4 tsp. vanilla

In a large bowl, sift together flour, sugar, soda, cinnamon and salt. Stir in apples, raisins, pecans, coconut and carrot: mix well. Beat eggs with oil and vanilla and stir into flour mixture until batter is just combined. Spoon batter into greased or paper-lined muffin tins, filling about 2/3 full.

Bake muffins in a preheated, 350-degree oven for 35 minutes or until they are springy to the touch.

Let muffins cool in tins on a rack for about 5 minutes, then remove muffins from tins; cool completely on rack.

Makes about 36 muffins.

Highlights of Joe Guilbault's 30-plus years in the hotel industry include opening and operating The Carlton, a five-star hotel in Johannesburg, South Africa (1970-1973), and the Peachtree Center Plaza in Atlanta (1973-1978). A senior vice president with the Stouffer Hotel Company, Joe was born in Helena, and he and his wife, Lucy, own a home on Flathead Lake.

GUTHRIE

The Barn • Star Route, Box 30 • Choteau, MT 59422

My husband, Bud, loved finding new recipes
or trying to re-create old ones he remembered from his boyhood in Choteau. Here are
two of his everyday favorites----both simple,
both good. The first he got from a chef
in a Hollywood restaurant. The second he
claimed to have invented.

CHIP BEEF ALA BANTAM

    2 C dried beef (rinse if too salty)
    ¼ C sliced mushrooms
    ½ C half-and half
    2 sliced avocados (fairly firm)
    ¼ C sliced almonds
Bring all ingredients just to a boil.
Simmer gently 10 minutes. Serve in patty
shells. Serves 4-6

DINNER IN A PAN

    4 pork chops, trimmed
    1 can tomatoes, chopped
    1 large onion, sliced
    1 green pepper, sliced
    ½ C rice
Brown chops. Add tomatoes, onion, green
pepper and rice to the pan. Season, cover,
and simmer for 30 to 40 minutes.
Serves 3-4

        Best of luck!

Carol Guthrie

Carol Guthrie

A.B. Guthrie, Jr., is the much loved and missed Pulitzer Prize–winning author, screen writer, scholar, and staunch environmentalist—who gave Montana its Big Sky nickname. His wife, Carol, who shared his recipes with us, lives in Choteau.

Levi Strauss & Co. Levi's Plaza, P.O. Box 7215, San Francisco, CA 94120 Phone 415 544-6000

I have really had two careers that have given me much pleasure and satisfaction. I was President and CEO of Levi Strauss & Co. for almost 20 years and am proud that our company is listed in the most recent *Fortune* magazine as the 5th most admired company in the U.S. Approaching retirement eleven years ago I bought a professional baseball team, the Oakland Athletics, which impresses my grandchildren's friends much more than my involvement with Levi's.

WALLY'S SPARERIB SAUCE

1 stick or 1/2 c. butter
3/4 c. catsup
1/2 c. brown sugar
3 T. lemon joice
1 T. Dijon style mustard
2 t. each of bottled steak sauce, hot pepper sauce (Tabasco), and Worcestershire sauce

Melt butter in saucepan. Stir in catsup, brown sugar, lemon juice, mustard, and steak, pepper and Worcestershire sauces.

We always put our ribs in a 375° oven for one half hour before putting on the sauce. This eliminates some of the spareribs' grease and fat. Therefore, to barbecue spareribs, first place in oven for half hour and then brush the ribs with sauce. Finally, put on grill and keep turning and basting. Cook for 45 minutes.

Among my greatest joys are the summers we spend at our ranch in Montana with my children and grandchildren. When we're at the ranch we fly a world's championship flag—probably the only one in Montana.

The above recipe is a favorite of ours—and we serve it at periodic barbecues for all the neighbors. Among the guests at an affair a couple of years ago were former President and Mrs. Jimmy Carter, who liked it as well.

Walter A. Haas, Jr.

Walter Haas, Jr., is past president of Levi Strauss and owner of a major league baseball team, the Oakland Athletics. He has a 3,500-acre ranch south of Big Timber near McLeod.

MARY HART'S CREAM CHEESE PIE

CRUST: 20 Graham crackers (crushed)
         1/3 Cup butter (melted)
         Pinch of salt

Mix together and put in a pie plate.
Bake 12 minutes at 350°

FILLING: 3/4 Cup sugar
         1 1/2 Large packages cream cheese (12 Ounces)
         2 Eggs beaten
         1 teaspoon vanilla

Mix together and pour into baked crust.
Bake 15 minutes at 350° - then let it Cool

TOPPING: Sour cream (small carton) 8 ounces or 1 Cup
         1/4 cup sugar
         1 teaspoon vanilla

Mix together and spread on top of pie and bake 7 minutes at 350°

Refrigerate several hours or overnight before serving.

TELEVISION DOMESTIC DISTRIBUTION

Mary Hart has been the hostess of Entertainment Tonight *since 1982. She and her husband, producer Burt Sugarman, own a home near Whitefish.*

TIM HAUCK
GREEN BAY PACKERS
1265 Lombardi Avenue
Green Bay, Wisconsin 54307

Since I have been known as a "Cookie Monster," below is a recipe that was one of my favorites, and also a favorite of my grandfather, John C. Hauck. When we would go to Butte, my Grandmother Betty, who was a wonderful cook, would fix these great cookies.

The chicken recipe is from the Grizzly Cookbook that was published while I was playing football at the University of Montana. It's a wonderful, easy meal. One even I can put together.

Oatmeal Crisps
1 c. butter, melted
1 c. brown sugar
1 c. flour
1 t. soda, dissolved in 1/4 c. boiling water
3 c. quick oats

Combine ingredients. Drop by spoonfuls and pat out very thin on a greased cookie sheet. Bake at 375° until good & brown.

Swiss Chicken
4 boned chicken breasts
4 slices processed Swiss cheese
1 can cream of chicken soup
1/4 can water
2 c. Pepperidge Farm stuffing mix
Melted butter

Place chicken breasts in casserole and cover wtih cheese slices. Combine soup & water; pour over cheese. Cover with stuffing. Drizzle melted butter over the top. Bake at 325° for 1 1/2 hours.

Good luck to the Intermountain Children's Home and all their dedicated workers.

Sincerely,

Tim C. Hauck

Tim Hauck was an all-state athlete in football, basketball and track from Big Timber. He is a free safety for the Green Bay Packers and was a two-time, First Team All-American while at the University of Montana. He was selected as Defensive MVP of the Big Sky Conference for two consecutive years.

BLACK BOTTOM CUPCAKES

These cupcakes are kind of tricky, but a lot of fun to make. I make them for birthdays and especially for my chocoholic friends. Be careful not to make them _too_ sweet. This recipe makes about 20 cupcakes, so give 15 and keep 5 for yourself.

Sift together:

1 1/2 cups of flour
1 cup of sugar
1 teaspoon of baking soda
1/2 cup of unsweetened chocolate
1/2 teaspoon of salt

In another bowl put:

1 cup water
5 tablespoons of oil
1 tablespoons of cider vinegar
1 teaspoon of vanilla

Mix all of the above and pour into cupcake papers half full.

Mix together:

8 ounces of cream cheese
1 egg
1/2 cup of sugar

Add six ounces of chocolate chips and put one huge tablespoon into each cupcake, right there on top.

Bake 20-25 minutes at 350 degrees and watch your calories for the rest of the day.

General Manager

The Helena Brewers joined the Pioneer League in 1978 as an affiliate of the Philadelphia Phillies, turned independent as the Gold Sox in 1984 and, since 1985, have been a Class A Short Season affiliate of the Milwaukee Brewers.

TRAVELS

THE SOUP JOHN HEMINWAY WISHES HE COULD CALL HIS OWN

The meals I remember best are ones consumed out in the open, preferably under stars, after a day of of exertion. It helps if there is a wind blowing and the crackling fire smells of acacia wood. At such times, nouvelle cuisine, cuisine minceur and tofu are rarely on our minds. If one is a poor sport one might wonder whether that lump in the soup is premeditated or a sausage beetle, bent on self-destruction. But protein is protein and, after a week on safari, everyone's a good sport.

The best food I ever had in the open was in East Africa and the Southern Sudan. Ingredients were generally fresh, the pressure lamps conveniently dim and the conversation always celestial. The best camp cook I ever encountered worked for some friends of mine in the north of Kenya-- in dry broken country filled with rhino and elephant. His real name was Andrea but everyone called him "Old Carry On"-- for his ability to produce miracles under the least forgiving conditions. His soups, prepared in advance, were invariably a tour de force. I include one that was transcribed orally since "Old Carry On" was better at remembering than writing.

I recommend this one for summer in Montana, the next best place to Africa.

OLD CARRY ON'S INSTANT BORSCH

4 smashed potatoes
4 cups pickled beets (cook beets with vinegar, cinnamon, cloves, onion and garlic)
2 chopped golden fried onions
4 tablespoons wine vinegar
4 teaspoons sugar
2 teaspoons salt
1 teaspoon hot pepper sauce
2 cups of beef broth

Put all ingredients in a blender, until smooth. Then chill. Top with horse radish and sour cream (3/4 cup sour cream and 2 teaspoon horseradish sauce).

John Heminway

John Heminway is the author of three books on Africa and executive producer and host of Travel, *on PBS. He has won an Emmy and a Peabody Award for Broadcast Journalism and is chairman of the board of the African Wildlife Foundation. He has a cattle ranch in the Bull Mountains as well as a fishing camp south of Livingston and Big Timber.*

Robert W. Hiatt
314 W. Dodge
Glendive, MT 59330

To refrigerate or not to refrigerate. — That is the question.

Gourmet and epicure are two nouns I am not. My palate deems a beef roast to be the ultimate in dining. One Monday late in my life the remainder of a Sunday roast was discovered on the counter unrefrigerated. That the flavor equaled that of the day before amazed and delighted me so much, I ate half of the sizable leftover. Tuesday I thoroughly enjoyed the second half with no sign of the meat "turning." Three days of great eating! I suspect but don't really know that that's the limit. I do know that I was never thrilled most of my lifetime with any cooked, then refrigerated beef. Since not a single woman that I've reported this to has even heard of such (and probably doesn't believe it), my only advice is: **Try it.** (You may love me forever after.)

But since that's not really a recipe, and to prove I'm not an "anti-refrigerationist," here goes with my late wife's recipe for my favorite **"Overnight Salad"**:

 1 head lettuce (cut up or torn with fingers)
 1/2 cup chopped celery
 1 cup chopped green pepper
 1 medium onion, chopped
 1 pkg. frozen peas, unthawed (I prefer "petite" peas.)
 1 cup mayonnaise
 2 tbsp. sugar
 4 oz. (about a cup) shredded cheddar cheese
 8 slices crisp bacon, crumbled

Layer the first 5 ingredients above in a 13 x 9 x 2 baking pan. Spread mayonnaise thereover. Sprinkle on sugar, cheese and bacon. Cover and refrigerate overnight. Toss before serving. (I've never tired of this recipe, and leftover salad covered in the fridge stays fresh for 2 or 3 days.)

Bob
Dr. R.W. Hiatt

As Dr. Robert Hiatt explains, "Glendive has been home the past two-thirds of my lifetime and the thought of leaving it has never entered my mind." He founded "The Only German Cowboy Band," and is an expert on and promoter of Makoshika State Park and the fossils found around it.

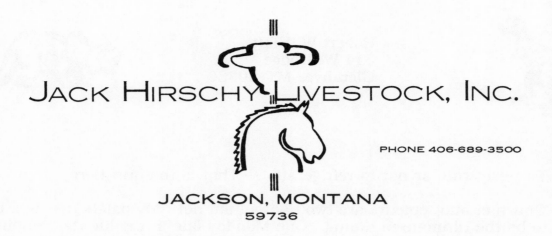

JACK HIRSCHY LIVESTOCK, INC.

PHONE 406-689-3500

JACKSON, MONTANA
59736

This is a good scalloped oyster recipe and I've been fixing them for our holiday dinners for over forty years, even though Jack and I never cared for them, most of our family and friends thought they were great!

SCALLOPED OYSTERS

1 pint oysters

2 cups medium-coarse cracker crumbs

½ cup butter or margarine, melted

½ teaspoon salt

3/4 cup light cream

¼ cup oyster liquor

¼ teaspoon Worcestershire sauce

Drain Oysters, reserving ¼ cup liquor. Combine crumbs, butter, salt. Spread 1/3 of crumbs in greased 8 x 1¼-inch round dish. Cover with half the oysters. Sprinkle with pepper. Using another third of the crumbs, spread a second layer; cover with remaining oysters. Sprinkle with pepper.

Combine cream, oyster liquor, Worcestershire sauce. Pour over the oysters. Top with last of crumbs. Bake in moderate oven (350) about 40 minutes. Makes 4 servings.

I usually triple this recipe to serve up to twenty people.

Ann Hirschy

In 1894, Jack Hirschy's grandparents homesteaded the Bighole Basin Ranch, starting a beef cattle and hay industry, which, over the past century, has supported five generations of Hirschys.

William Hjortsberg
Main Boulder Route
McLeod, Montana 59052

BABA GHANNOOJ

I first developed a taste for Middle Eastern food during my undergraduate years at Dartmouth in the early 1960s. There, at Lander's Restaurant, located appropriately enough in West Lebanon, New Hampshire, I first became acquainted with the mysteries of hummus, dolmas and kibbi. In time, I discovered that these exotic delicasies were in reality simple dishes to prepare and I've been making and enjoying them ever since.

For quite a while, I resisted attempting the recipe included here because I was told that in order to be authentic one must roast the eggplants over a charcoal fire on a sharpened stick. This is how it's done in Anatolia. In Montana, it just didn't seem worth the trouble, until I came up with a method compatible with both authenticity and modern kitchens:

         2   medium-sized eggplants
         3   tablespoons sesame tahina paste
         2   tablespoons finely-chopped garlic
         ½   cup olive oil
             juice of 2 lemons
             ground cumin (to taste, I like at least 3 Tbs)
             ground cayenne (to taste)

Cut the eggplants in half lengthwise and place them, skin side up, in a metal baking dish containing ½ inch of water.

Place the baking dish in the oven so that the tops of the eggplants are about 5 inches below the broiler flame. Broil them for approximately 20 minutes, or until the skins are charred and the insides are steamed to a soft consistency.

Drain well and place the cooked eggplants, together with all the other ingredients, in a food processor. Use the standard blade and process until the whole is a soft paste.

Serve as an appetizer with pita bread cut into wedge-shaped sections.

William Hjortsberg

William Hjortsberg has published six books of fiction, including the novel, Falling Angel, *which was the basis of the film,* Angel Heart. *Also among his screen credits is the script (and original story) for* Legend, *directed by Ridley Scott. He has a home in the Big Timber/McLeod area.*

j. d. holmes

RE: RECIPE FROM J.D. HOLMES

TURKEY DIVAN
(Serves Eight)

One 6-0z. package stuffing mix for turkey

Two 10-oz. packages frozen broccoli spears

Eight large slices cooked turkey

Two 11-oz. cans condensed Cheddar Cheese soup

One-half cup milk

Two tablespoons minced green onion

Two tablespoons chopped pimento

Cook broccoli, drain thoroughly.
Place eight mounds of cooked stuffing mix
in a greased 13 by 9-inch baking dish.
Cover each mound with a turkey slice, then broccoli.
Combine remaining ingredients, pour over broccoli.
Bake at 400 degrees for 25-30 minutes.

My wife, Bert, says this makes a great luncheon,
served with a hot roll and several slices of fresh
fruit.

But I hasten to add that it's also a great match-making
tool. We had a couple over for dinner one night and
hoped they would become good friends.

Turkey Divan was the entree that evening and the
couple's friendship still blooms after a year or so.

Sincerely,

J. D. Holmes.

512 north rodney • helena, montana 59601 • (406) 442-3258

J.D. Holmes was the Associated Press state capital reporter for Montana for 30 years. He lives in Helena.

20-30 lb. Roast from the Underground

1. Dig a hole 3' deep x 3' wide

2. Line the hole with rock (bottom and sides)

3. Build a big wood fire in the hole (Need 4" of coals at bottom)

4. While fire is going, build an aluminum foil pan to hold roast

5. Sprinkle a package of onion soup mix over the roast and add 1/2 cup of water

6. Wrap aluminum foil pan and roast in aluminum foil (seal completely)

7. Wrap this package in burlap and tie up with heavy string or light rope

8. While coals are hot, cover them with 2-3" of dirt

9. Place roast package in hole on the dirt

10. Cover the roast pack with dirt--about 3" over top of package

11. Build second fire on top
    Either keep this fire going for about 4 hours or bury the coals and put in corn on the cob, potatoes, etc. wrapped in aluminum foil, and then cover and build a third fire.

12. After 4 hours dig up everything and enjoy a very moist Dino-dinner!

One day each summer the Museum of the Rockies Dino Diggers have a special dinner. All the field crews get together and cook a beef or bison roast. Dinner preparations take all day, but it's great fun and truly an underground feast.

Jack Horner

Jack Horner

Jack Horner was born in Shelby. He is one of the world's leading paleontologists, and is curator at the Museum of the Rockies in Bozeman. His findings have changed the world's views on dinosaurs.

ARCHBISHOP
RAYMOND G. HUNTHAUSEN

ARCHDIOCESE OF SEATTLE
910 MARION STREET
SEATTLE, WASHINGTON 98104
(206) 382-4884

A PRIEST'S STEAK

Sprinkle both sides of steak with Johnny's Tenderizer, pour and spread both sides of steak with Kitchen Bouquet, repeat with Heinz 57 Steak Sauce. Marinate 3 hours. Season and broil to taste.

AN ARCHBISHOP'S STEAK

Spread steak with pure lemon juice. Follow with prepared mustard. Let marinate overnight. Season and broil to taste.

AN ARCHBISHOP'S SUNDAE

Pour creme de menthe over vanilla ice cream.

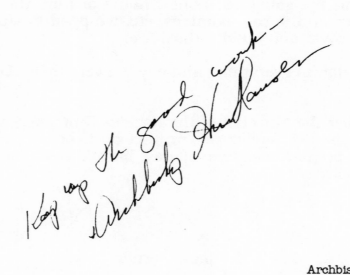

Archbishop Raymond G. Hunthausen

Archbishop Raymond G. Hunthausen was born in Anaconda, ordained to the priesthood in 1946, consecrated Bishop of Helena in 1962, and appointed Archbishop of Seattle in 1975. He retired in 1991. He was a professor, athletic director and president of Carroll College.

HUCKLEBERRY CHICKEN

Here is an easy to prepare recipe which has been an Inn favorite for over 9 years.

1- 5 oz. chicken breast,boneless,grilled; served on top of fettucini in a cream sauce-(recipe follows).Pour one oz. of Huckleberry sauce over the chicken breast. Serve with side dish of fresh vegetables--your choice.

Huckleberry sauce:
1 cup water
1 cup huckleberries
3/4 cup sugar
1 tbl.cornstarch
1/8 teas. salt
1 teas. lemon juice

Boil water,add huckleberries. In a small bowl, combine sugar,cornstarch, salt. Stir into berries, and cook until thickened. Add lemon juice.

Fettucini sauce:

1 cup real butter
2 cups flour
4 cups milk
1/8 tsp. granulated garlic
1 qt. whipping cream
1 cup white wine
Melt butter, then add the flour to form a roux. Add the 4 cups milk and blend until smooth and thickened. Add garlic, whipping cream and wine. Blend and cook until correct consistency.

Approximately 6 servings

Picking huckleberries is a special event for the Vielleux family. After convincing our 6 year old granddaughter that frills, dresses, and lace are not the appropriate attire for picking, we are off to pick as she calls them "hucklebabies".

Larry Vielleux

P.O. Box 653
Essex, Montana 59916
Phone: 406 888-5700

Izaak Walton Inn is snuggled between Glacier National Park and the Bob Marshall Wilderness. This 30-room hotel, built in 1939, offers a haven for cross-country skiers, hikers, fishermen, hunters and railroad enthusiasts.

JIMMY LEE'S Chinese Restaurant

6550 Hwy. 93 South
Whitefish, MT 59937
(406) 862-5303

James Lee Laidlaw

As a young boy in the early 1950's, I grew up in Taipei, Taiwan. One of our favorite places to eat was the Grand Hotel, owned by the wife of Chiang Kai Shek the President of the Republic of China. When I first started Jimmy Lee's, the dishes I served came from recipes I learned from my mother who attended Chinese cooking classes at the Grand Hotel which is still a landmark hotel and restaurant in Taipei.

BEEF & GREEN PEPPER
(serves 2)

Ingredients:

8 oz.	Beef sirloin (sliced paper thin)
4 oz.	Green pepper (sliced)
1 Tbsp.	Fresh ginger (peeled & sliced)
3 ea.	Green onions (cut white part in 1" pieces)
1 Tbsp.	Liquid oil

"Marinating" Sauce:

4 Tbsp.	Chicken broth (Swansons)
1 tsp.	Baking powder
1 Tbsp.	Soy sauce
1/2 tsp.	Salt
1 tsp.	Corn starch

"Frying" Sauce:

5 Tbsp.	Chicken Broth
1/2 tsp.	Salt
1 tsp.	Corn Starch
2 tsp.	Sesame oil
2 tsp.	Sugar

Method of Cooking:

Measure out the ingredients and prepare the "marinating" and "frying" sauces and put these aside.

Using your fingers, mix the sliced beef with the "marinating" sauce. Using a wok or deep frying pan, heat 2 cups of oil to a high heat. Put the marinated beef into the pan and deep fry the beef for about 1 minute. Remove beef from the wok from the fire and drain the oil.

Put the wok back on the stove and add 1 Tbsp. of oil. When hot, add the green pepper, ginger and green onions. Lastly add the beef and the "frying" sauce and cook for 1 or 2 minutes until thickened.

Jimmy Lee's restaurant in Whitefish draws people from all over the Flathead Valley with its wonderful Cantonese and Szechwan food. One of the most popular recipes is called "Jimmy's Lunch," a recipe combining ingredients from many cultures. It is actually a dinner served in a big bowl.

LYNN "JONNIE" JONCKOWSKI   BILLINGS,MT.

SWEET AND SOUR MEAT BALLS

meat balls-

1 lb. venison hamburger
1/2 c. dry bread crumbs
1/4 c. skim milk
2 tbs. finely chopped onion
1 tsp. salt
1 egg

mix- shape into small balls and cook over medium heat turning
occasionally until brown.

sweet & sour sauce-

1/2 c. packed brown sugar
1 tbs cornstarch
1 can pineapple chunks (13oz.)
1 tbs. soy sauce
1 small green pepper chopped
1/3 cup vinegar

mix- brown sugar and cornstarch in skillet. Stir in pineapple, vinegar
and soy sauce. Heat to a boil stir always. Add meat balls, cover and
simmer 10 minutes. Add green peppers, cover another 10 minutes, stir
once more just before serving.

Serve with rice, tossed salad and your favorite beverage.

This is my favorite dinner when I come off the road. Its a great way
to make montana venison into a gourmet meal. YUMMMMMM........
I suppose that venison from another state would work equally as well.
If you must, I suppose beef would even work but that is so normal.

*Lynn "Jonnie" Jonckowski is a two-time world champion bull rider (1986 and 1988), spokeswoman, model and movie
consultant. Lynn was named Woman of the '80s by CNN, and she makes her home in Billings.*

Elsie Jones
Governor's Mansion
2 Carson
Helena, Montana 59601

ORANGE SUPREME DESSERT

Dissolve one large package and one small package of orange jello in 1 1/2 cups boiling water. Set aside. In a separate bowl, combine one small can of crushed pineapple, 1 1/2 cups fresh orange juice with pulp, the juice of one lemon, and 1 1/2 cups sugar. Allow the orange juice and lemon to set for about 10 minutes, then stir until the sugar is dissolved.

Add orange juice mixture to the gelatin mixture. Let stand until mixture begins to thicken. Blend in 1 1/2 cups whipped cream. Set aside.

Break up one angel food cake and place pieces evenly in a 9 by 13 oblong pan. Layer with 1 1/2 cups miniature marshmallows, then 3/4 cup chopped pecans, then gelatin mixture. Refrigerate. When ready to serve, add whipped cream and garnish with orange slices and coconut. Serves 8.

CHICKEN RICE CASSEROLE

1 1/2 lbs. cooked chicken breast
1/2 cup rice that has been cooked ten minutes and drained
3 cups chicken broth
1 tablespoon chopped green pepper
2 tablespoon chopped onion
1/2 cup chopped water chestnuts
3/4 cup chopped celery
1/4 cup chopped mushrooms
1/4 cup cashews

Chop cooked chicken breast into bite-size pieces Mix chicken with onion, green pepper, celery, mushrooms, cashews, rice, water chestnuts and chicken broth. Place mixture into 2-quart casserole dish and bake for 35-40 minutes at 350 degrees. Sprinkle crushed potato chips on top just before serving. Serves 6 to 8.

Elsie Jones, from East Helena, is the longest-serving state employee in the United States. She has been housekeeper and cook for Montana's last eight governors. She first worked for Governor John Bonner in 1948.

— 92 —

SKIWEAR

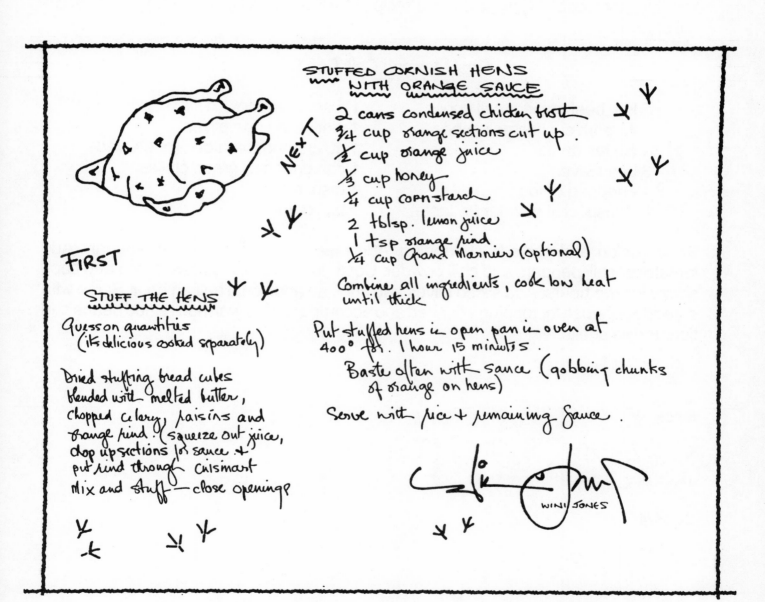

STUFFED CORNISH HENS WITH ORANGE SAUCE

2 cans condensed chicken broth
¾ cup orange sections cut up.
½ cup orange juice
⅓ cup honey
¼ cup corn starch
2 tblsp. lemon juice
1 tsp orange rind
¼ cup Grand Marnier (optional)

Combine all ingredients, cook low heat until thick

Put stuffed hens in open pan in oven at 400° for 1 hour 15 minutes.
  Baste often with sauce (gobbing chunks of orange on hens)

Serve with rice + remaining sauce.

WINI JONES

NEXT

FIRST

STUFF THE HENS

Guess on quantities
(its delicious cooked separately)

Dried stuffing bread cubes
blended with melted butter,
chopped celery, raisins and
orange rind. (squeeze out juice,
chop up sections for sauce +
put rind through cuisinart
Mix and stuff — close openings

Wini Jones, a University of Montana graduate, is vice president of Roffe Skiwear and the only skiwear designer ever nominated to the prestigious Council of Fashion Designers of America. She has been instrumental in developing innovative fabrics for the active-wear market.

THOMAS L. JUDGE COMPANY

801 NORTH MAIN

POST OFFICE BOX 815

HELENA, MONTANA 59624-0815

TELEPHONE (406) 443-2064
FACSIMILE (406) 449-3668

Your idea for a book is great. This is a recipe that Suzie and I love. I hope your readers will enjoy it.

Real Mexican Chili Con Carne

2 lbs. beef cut in small cubes
1 lb. pork cut in small cubes
4 cloves garlic
3 bay leaves
1 chopped onion
2-3 tbsp. chili powder (to taste)

1 tbsp. oregano
1 pint sliced ripe olives
1 qt. canned tomatoes (or stewed)
1 can chopped green chilies
1 tbsp. salt
1 tsp. cumin

Brown onion and garlic in shortening. Add meat; cover and cook thoroughly. Add tomatoes, chili peppers and chili powder. Cook 20 minutes. Add seasoning and cook slowly for two hours. Add sliced olives and cook an additional half an hour. Serve with shredded cheese for topping if desired and accompanied by warmed refried beans and flour tortilla shells.

Sincerely,

Thomas L. Judge

SJ:ps/jr

Tom Judge was Montana's two-term governor from 1973 through 1981. Governor Judge worked his way up the political ladder serving in the Montana House of Representatives and the Montana Senate, and as Lieutenant Governor. Today he is an investment broker. He and his wife, Suzie, have a home in Helena and one in Bigfork.

JULIANO'S RESTAURANT

WHITE CHOCOLATE MOUSSE WITH FRANGELICO

8 oz. white chocolate, broken into small pieces
1/2 cup (1 stick) unsalted butter
6 eggs, separated, room temperature
1 cup sifted confectioners' sugar
1/2 cup Frangelico liqueur
2 cups whipping cream, cold
Pinch of cream of tartar
Unsweetened cocoa powder or grated dark chocolate (garnish)

Melt the white chocolate and butter in a small saucepan, stirring constantly. Set aside.
Beat the egg yolks, sugar, and liqueur until the mixture forms a slowly dissolving ribbon when the beaters are lifted. Pour the mixture into the top of a double boiler and cook, whisking constantly, over simmering water until very thick, about 3 minutes.

Remove to a large mixing bowl. Whisk in the white chocolate mixture and stir until smooth and cool.

Beat the cream until the peaks are stiff. In a separate bowl with clean beaters, beat the egg whites with the cream of tartar until stiff but not dry. Gently fold the egg whites into the chocolate mixture; then fold in the whipped cream. Refrigerate covered until set, about 3 hours.
Spoon the chilled mousse into individual ramekins or goblets. Sprinkle with cocoa or grated chocolate.
10 to 12 portions

Jan Louise

2912 7th Avenue North
Billings, Montana
248-6400

Owned and managed by Jan Redies since 1986, Juliano's in Billings is one of Montana's most elegant gourmet restaurants. The exquisite meals served are deserving of its five-star rating, the only one in Montana.

Michael Keaton

Every Christmas a friend, "Mama" Goldberg sends me
a variety of scrumptious home baked goodies. Here's
one of my favorites:

LEMON SQUARES

1 cup flour
1/2 cup powdered sugar
2 cubes (either 1 cube margarine and 1 cube butter,
         or 2 cubes butter)

Mix the sugar and flour and then cut into this the
margarine and butter. Pat this mixture in a 13" x 9"
pan and build the sides up all around about 1" high.

Bake this for 20-25 minutes at 350 degrees.

Beat and mix together:

4 eggs
1 1/2 cups of regular sugar
4 tablespoons of flour
1/2 cup of lemon juice (you may want to add more,
         depending on how tart you like this)
Grate the entire lemon and add the rind to this
         mixture.

When the above crust is finished, then pour this
lemon mixture over it. Then bake again for 15-20
minutes at 350 degrees.

Take out of the oven, let it cool and cut into
1 1/2 inch squares. They're yummy...............

Michael Keaton is an actor whose movies include Mr. Mom, Johnny Dangerously, Gung Ho, Beetlejuice, Dream Team, Batman, One Good Cop *and* Batman Returns. *An avid sports fan, he is involved in charity work and owns a ranch in the Big Timber/McLeod area.*

Lasagne for a bunch

2 16 oz. pkgs. Lasagne noodles
2 to 3 lbs. lean Montana ground beef

2 large jars of your favorite spaghetti sauce

mushrooms & onions

big tub   sour cream
big tub   cottage cheese
parsley
2 lbs. low fat mozzarella cheese

Brown ground beef. Saute mushrooms & onions & combine.
Add sauce.   Boil your noodles up and then start layer process.

A big aluminum turkey roasting pan or big baking dish is what you need.

On the bottom start with the meat mixture.
Then noodles.
Cheese (you can grate or slice) and cottage cheese and sour cream.
Noodles.
Sauce
Noodles
Sauce
How many ever layers you'd like.

Bake at 300 to 350° for 50 to 60 minutes. Let it sit before you serve.

Really even better as flavors mix when you can make and bake night before
and then next day heat it thru and dish it up!

Add garlic as friends and family will stand. We like lots! It's supposed
to be good for you!

Donna Kelley

Donna Kelley is a CNN anchorwoman and co-host of International Hour. *She has been associated with CNN since 1984. She was born in Havre and lived in Bozeman.*

MONTANA BEVERAGES, LTD.

1439 Harris Street
Helena, Montana 59601
406/449-6214
FAX 406/449-8119

Brewers of
KESSLER BEER

MONTANA'S PREMIUM
LAGER BEER

Dear Friends of Intermountain Children's Home:

I acquired my love of German-style beer and premium wines during the three years that I lived in Europe following a tour of Germany thanks to the U.S. Army. It was this exposure that led me to the premium wine import and distribution business and finally to be co-founder of the Kessler Brewing Company, brewers of many fine German-style beers.

The love of fine wines and beer quickly led to the appreciation of European-style meals. Gourmet cooking soon became an additional hobby, combined with a passion for using only the freshest ingredients.

This is a recipe I discovered years ago when I was courting the lovely lady who is now my wife. This meal stands out in my mind as perhaps having helped get her attention. We still enjoy it often—although, I must admit, most of the time she now prepares it.

Sautéed Chicken Breasts in Lemon Cream

1 1/2 c. heavy cream
Juice of one medium lemon
6 T. unsalted butter
3/4 lb. fresh mushrooms, sliced
3 whole chicken breasts
(about 1 lb. ea.), skinned, boned, halved
Salt
Freshly-ground white pepper
All-purpose flour

1 onion, halved
1 clove garlic
1 bay leaf
1 c. chicken broth
2 c. fresh or frozen peas

1. Mix cream and lemon juice; reserve.

2. Heat 3 T. of the butter in large skillet over medium-high heat until foam subsides. Sauté mushrooms in butter, half at a time, until nicely browned; removed with slotted spoon; reserve.

3. Salt and pepper chicken breasts; dredge lightly with flour, shaking off excess. Add remaining 3 T. butter and the oil to the skillet; heat until hot. Add onion halves, cut side down. Brown chicken over medium heat, about 5 minutes per side. Remove chicken from skillet. Remove and discard all but 1 T. of the fat.

4. Add broth and bay leaf to skillet. Crush garlic clove with flat side of large knife and add. Heat till boiling; reduce liquid to 3/4 cup. Remove and discard onion and bay leaf. Reduce heat to medium; add reserved lemon-cream mixture. Cook, stirring frequently with wire whisk, until sauce is thick and reduce to 2 cups. Return mushrooms and chicken to skillet. Simmer, spooning sauce over chicken, until chicken is heated through, and chicken is no longer pink in center, approximately 4 to 5 minutes. Add peas and heat until peas are just warm. Garnish with the parsley. Serve with Rice Pilaf.

Rice Pilaf

2 T. unsalted butter
1 small onion, finely minced
1 c. brown long-grain rice
1 t. salt

pepper to taste
2 1/4 c. chicken broth
1 T. minced parsley
1 clove garlic, minced and sautéed

Heat butter in medium-heavy saucepan. Add onion; cook over low heat, stirring frequently, until soft but not brown, about 5 minutes. Add rice; stir to coat completely with butter. Stir in salt and pepper. Add broth; heat to boiling; reduce heat. Simmer, covered, until rice is tender, approximately 40 minutes. Gently fold in parsley and garlic (if desired).

This dish is best served with some crusty sour-dough bread and, of course, a white wine from the Burgundy region of France, or, if you must, a California Chardonnay—preferable from the Carneros region. Enjoy!

Sincerely,

Bruce H. DeRosier, CEO
Montana Beverages, Ltd.

The Kessler Brewery was started in Helena in the late 1800s and closed in the 1950s. Bruce DeRosier and Dick Bourke, in 1984, opened a new brewery with the old name. Besides Kessler beer they brew award-winning private-label beers for distributors and entrepreneurs.

LOYD KETCHUM

Box 1053 • Miles City, MT • 59301
Phone: 406/232-3873
PRCA # C20056M

When we was batching in high school we were quite the cooks.
This recipe was something that Richard Sparks and myself
had whip together, so when we got done with basketball practice
the crockpot had it all done for us. Of course when I am
cooking I like to have a good selection of this and that and
some spices. Richard and I decided to call this specialty
GORP!!

                    GORP
        1lb Hamburger
        1 or 2 cans of green cut beans
        1 or 2 cans of porken beans
        1 onion
        This and that

Seemed to be best to brown the hamburger. This is where to
get into the spices. Be sure to use some minced onions or
if have time to let your eyes water, cut up 1 small whole
onion, salt pepper, this and that, and whatever else sounds
good. Mix all into the browning hamburger.

After browning is done, put into the crockpot, add the green
beans with most of the juice and the porken beans. Stir,
let simmer rest of the day. Be ready at night. Probably even
better warmed up the next day.

GORP!! How we came by the name of GORP, neither of us seem
too remember, I guess the name sounded good at the time. If
you get the nerve to try this recipe, hope you get the right
this and that, because if you get the wrong this and that,
it could mean GORP!! Gotto run poop!!

---

*Loyd Ketchum was a three-sport standout at Plevna High School. As a member of the Miles City Community College
Rodeo Team, he participated in every event except bareback riding. He was named 1991 World Champion Wrangler
Bullfighter at the National Finals Rodeo and he lives in Miles City.*

Mimi Kiser

Thanks very much for including me as a contributor to the "Montana Celebrity Cookbook." Like so many people, I come from a dysfunctional family, and feel that this fund raiser is for an especially important cause. One can never under-estimate how important it is that all children grow up in a stable and loving environment. These kids are our future.

CAVIAR PIE TORTE

    9" spring form pan
    4 pkgs. cream cheese
    1/2 pint sour cream
    1/2 cup chopped onions and/or scallions
    6 hard boiled eggs, chopped
    1 large jar of caviar (preferably paddlefish caviar from Glendive)

Mix cream cheese and sour cream in a bowl and spread half of mixture in the bottom of the pan. Layer with 1/2 cup of onions/scallions. Then layer this with all of the chopped eggs. Top with remaining cream mixture and put in refrigerator to set for an hour. Drain caviar and spread on top. Garnish with parsley and serve with Bremmer wafers or any light cracker.

If you love caviar, this makes a great hors d'oeuvre. I stole this recipe from a friend in Denver and first made it in Montana for a road trip through Yellowstone with some realtor friends. Our intention was to celebrate a then recent land purchase. One of my friends, being a true meat-eating Montanan, refused to touch the torte. And, instead of bringing champagne, brought the makings for a McLeod Silver Devil (don't ask). At least it left more for the rest of us!

CAUTION: Do not bring this dish on any road trip and do not ingest with Silver Devils. It will be messy, otherwise.

Mimi Kiser

Mimi Ki

Mimi Kiser, an "escaped" actress from Los Angeles and New York City, now lives in the McLeod area. Her work includes stage roles, a part on television's The Young and The Restless, *and a featured role in the film version of* A River Runs Through It.

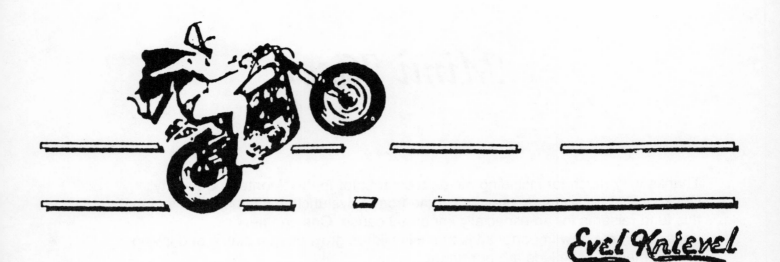

GREEN RICE

2 EGGS, BEATEN
1 LARGE CAN SEGO MILK
1/3 CUP SALAD OIL

BEAT TOGETHER

ADD 2 CUPS BOILED RICE
1 CLOVE GARLIC
1 SMALL ONION, MINCED
1/3 CUP CHOPPED PARSLEY
1/2 TO 1 LB. SHARP CHEESE, MINCED
SALT & PEPPER TO TASTE

BAKE 50 MIN., UNCOVERED, 350°, GREASED 2QT. CASSEROLE

THIS IS ONE OF MY FAVORITE DISHES BAKED BY MY
GRANDMOTHER, WHO RAISED ME. SHE TURNED 98, NOV. 1991.

Evel Knievel

EVEL KNIEVEL

Evel Knievel, from Butte, is a retired daredevil motorcycle stuntman who made many incredible jumps including a most spectacular one over the fountain at Caesars Palace. His son Robbie continues in his father's tradition today.

Bill Kollar, Assistant Coach

BANANA CREAM PIE

2/3 cup sugar
1/2 tsp salt
2-3 T cornstarch
2 1/2 T flour
2 1/4 C milk
2 large egg yolks
1 tsp butter
1 tsp vanilla

8-inch pie crust, baked and cooled
bananas
1/2 pint whipping cream
confectioners' sugar
vanilla

Mix sugar, salt, cornstarch, and flour in saucepan. Gradually stir in milk and cook over moderate heat, stirring constantly until mixture thickens and boils. Boil one minute.

Remove from heat and slowly stir one-half of mixture into egg yolks. Blend egg-yolk mixture back into mixture remaining in saucepan. Boil one minute, stirring. Remove from heat. Blend in butter and vanilla. Cool, stirring occasionally. Do not cover.

Slice a couple of bananas into empty baked shell and pour cooled mixture into shell. Chill two hours.

Whip cream and add vanilla and confectioners' sugar to taste. Top pie with whipped cream and more sliced bananas.

Banana cream pie is my favorite and my wife makes the best. This is her recipe. When she makes a banana cream pie, I cut it in half and eat one of the halves as my first piece.

Bill Kollar

Bill Kollar graduated from Montana State University in 1958, and lived in Bozeman during the off-season while he played football for the Cincinnati Bengals and the Tampa Bay Buccaneers. He is now assistant coach for the Atlanta Falcons. He and his wife, Jan, get to Montana as often as possible.

HUEY LEWIS

Well, here goes:

Duck with Peppercorn Sauce

4 duck breasts
2 t. peppercorns (green)
1 T. currant jelly
1 onion (chopped)
1 bay leaf
1/2 c. chopped parsley stems
1 bottle red burgundy wine
1 pint heavy cream

Marinate the duck breasts in a saucepan of red wine, parsley stems and chopped onion and one bay leaf for about 4 hours or more. Remove breasts and reduce marinade over high heat, slowly adding heavy cream, currant jelly and green peppercorns until sauce begins to thicken.
Grill the breasts in olive oil or barbecue them, being careful to leave them pink on the inside. Slice the breasts in about 1/2" thick slices, arrange them on the plate and smother with the peppercorn sauce.

Congratulations on your very good cause.

Huey Lewis is a singer, composer and lead vocalist for the band Huey Lewis and the News. The Grammy-winning band's hits include Hip to Be Square, Want a New Drug, Small World *and* Back in Time. *He owns a home in the Bitterroot Valley.*

Bud Lilly

(406) 586-5140

2007 Sourdough Road
Bozeman, MT 59715

VANILLA ICE CREAM

Separate 8 eggs.

Beat whites until nearly stiff.

Carefully add:
    Egg yolks
    4 quarts half and half
      or ranch cream
    2 3/4 cups sugar
    8 tsp vanilla
    1/2 tsp salt

Place mixture in home hand freezer
cannister and refrigerate overnight.

Next day, hand crank until solid
ice cream is formed. Eat at once
alone or with others.

My mother Violet craved ice cream during
her pregnancy with me. The craving
with me has been a factor in choosing
fishing accesses near ice cream stands.

BUD LILLY

Bud Lilly, Montana's most famous fly fisherman, owned The Trout Shop in West Yellowstone for 30 years. An expert fly fishing instructor, he was named 1991 Fly Fishing Guide of the Year by Rod & Reel Magazine. Bud now lives in Bozeman.

INTERNATIONAL SKI FEDERATION

INTERNATIONALER SKI-VERBAND

FÉDÉRATION INTERNATIONALE DE SKI

A. R. (BUD) LITTLE M.D.
1019 FLOWERREE STREET
HELENA, MONTANA 59601
U.S.A.

The following are from a collection of family recipes.

Chocolate Corn Flake Cookies

1 package (small) chocolate chips melted in double boiler with 2 T. peanut butter; take off heat. Toss in 2 cups corn flakes or Rice Krispies and drop onto a cookie sheet, with or without waxed paper, piled up to a point. Let stand until dry.

A Nice Dessert

Mix 1 pound small marshmallows and 1 small can pineapple chunks. Next day add ½ to 1 cup chopped nuts and ½ pint whipped cream. Cool and serve.

Dr. Carson's Receipt to relieve a person whose stomach is craving for alcoholic liquor. From Grandma Markoe's receipt book—1800.

One oz. of wormwood to 1 pt. of water. Strain it and take a wineglass full 4 times a day.
When the weather is very hot or the person appears to be exhausted put in quietly a tablespoonful (three cheers for grandma) of whiskey. The temperature is now 110° in the shade.

Dr. Amos "Bud" Little, a Helena physician, was vice president of the International Ski Federation for many years, and has been involved with the Olympics officially since 1957, when he was asked to manage the 1960 U.S. Olympic ski team.

MIKE AND SHIRLEY OWENS
Livingston Bar & Grille
130 North Main St.
Livingston, MT 59047
222-7909

We are sharing our favorite and most popular recipe. This is the only recipe we have refused to give out in the past.

STUFFED JALAPENOS

1 lb. can lightly pickled whole jalapenos
4 cups medium shrimp, cut in pieces
6 tablespoons butter
6 tablespoons flour
2 cups onions, finely minced
2 cups green onions, finely chopped
⅔ cup heavy cream with 2 tablespoons chicken soup base (powder)
¼ cup white wine
2 tablespoons lemon juice
½ cup parsley flakes
1 teaspoon white pepper
1½ teaspoon cayenne pepper
2 teaspoons garlic in oil
1½ cups mushrooms, finely chopped
1¼ cups bread crumbs, fine
1 teaspoon Tabasco
Salt to taste

Egg and Milk Mixture:

3 eggs
1 quart milk

Whip together until smoothly blended.

Make light roux with butter and flour (melt butter in large skillet and add flour. Cook on high for 3 minutes, constantly stirring). Add all ingredients except Tabasco, salt and bread crumbs. Simmer for 10 minutes. Add remaining ingredients. Mixture must be thick enough for stuffing. If needed, add more bread crumbs. Remove from heat and let cool. Use canned, lightly pickled whole jalapenos. Cut each jalapeno open and spoon out seeds. Spread open and spoon stuffing into jalapeno. Mold into oblong shape about the size of a very small egg. Roll first in flour, egg and milk mixture, then in bread crumbs. Deep fry until golden brown. Serve with tartar sauce.

This recipe makes about 30-40 stuffed jalapenos. They freeze well. After breading, lay out on a cookie sheet, set in your freezer until hardened, then box or bag as desired. When cooking frozen, thaw in microwave for 1½ minutes on high, then deep fry.

Mike & Shirley Owens

Livingston Bar and Grille in Livingston was included on Esquire *magazine's literary map of the cosmos and boasts a 100-year-old hand-carved backbar from France. Mike and Shirley Owens' Louisiana background is reflected in their recipes.*

LONE MOUNTAIN RANCH

P.O. Box 69   Big Sky, MT 59716
(406) 995-4644

BOB'S SPICY BLACK BEAN SOUP

1/2 lb.	Dried Black Beans
1-3	Fresh destemmed and deseeded Jalapenos, finely chopped (1 if you like to keep it mild, and 2 or 3 if you like more heat!)
2 Tblsp.	Olive Oil
3 Cloves	Garlic, finely chopped
2	Medium Onions, coarsely chopped
2	14-1/2 oz. cans of Beef Broth
1 Tblsp.	Ground New Mexico Red Chili (not chili powder)
1	small meaty Ham Hock, or 2 smoked Turkey Wings
1 tsp.	Ground Cumin
2 tsp.	Dried Oregano
1	Bay Leaf
1/4 cup	Dry Red Wine

Salt to taste and garnish with chopped Cilantro, chopped Green Onions and shredded Cheddar Cheese.

Wash the beans and soak them overnight by covering with about 3 inches of water. Drain the beans. Heat olive oil in a pan and saute the garlic and onions for 3-4 minutes. Add the broth, beans, ham hock or turkey wings, ground New Mexico chili, and bay leaf. Simmer for 2 hours. Add the jalapenos, cumin, oregano and red wine and simmer for another 2 hours. Thicken by removing half a cup of the beans and blending or mashing them and stirring them back into the pot. Remove the meat from the ham hock or turkey wings and add to the soup. Add salt to taste, and garnish as you serve.

Bob Schaap

LONE MOUNTAIN RANCH
P.O. Box 69   Big Sky, MT 59716
(406) 995-4644

Montana Huckleberry Chocolate Fleck Pie

What better way to combine two wonderful foods -- chocolate and Montana Huckleberries! This is a great desert to make a few days before needed and a favorite for Christmas dinner!

Pie Crust

Combine 1/2 cup butter and 2 Tblsp. sugar. Do not cream. Add 1 cup flour. Mix just until dough will form. Place 1/4 cup of mixture crumbled in small pan. Press remaining mixture evenly over bottom and sides of 9 inch pie pan with well floured fingers. Bake at 375° until light golden brown. Bake crumbs 10-12 minutes and crust 12-15 minutes.

Pie Filling

Melt 1/2 cup semi-sweet Chocolate Chips in double boiler. Cool to lukewarm.

Combine in small bowl:
   2/3 cup Sugar
   1/4 cup Water
   1 unbeaten Egg White
   1-1/2 tsp. Vanilla
   1 tsp. Lemon Juice

Beat with electric mixer at highest speed until soft peaks form when beaters are raised (3-5 minutes). Beat 1 cup whipping cream until thick. Fold melted chocolate slowly into whipped cream mixture then fold into egg white mixture. Fold 1/2 cup of huckleberries into the mixture. Put into pie crust and freeze.

Enjoy!

Vivian Schaap

Vivian Schaap

Lone Mountain Guest Ranch at Big Sky is one of the top six cross-country ski resorts in the nation. In the summer it is a family dude ranch. Owners Bob and Vivian Schaap and Mike Ankeny provide great food, atmosphere and service that keeps guests returning each year.

A Division of
COTTONWOOD
GRAPHICS, INC.
1-800-937-6343

(406) 862-2620

P.O. Box 848
410 East Second Street
Whitefish, MT 59937-0484
(406) 862-6343
FAX: (406) 862-2898

ELEANOR LYNDE'S APPLE CRISP

Submitted with gratitude by her son, Stan

1 QT. APPLES, SLICED OR CHOPPED
¼ CUP WATER
½ CUP SUGAR
1 TEASPOON CINNAMON

Sprinkle apples with water, sugar, and cinnamon.

Blend 1 CUP BROWN SUGAR
      ¼ CUP BUTTER
      ¼ CUP FLOUR

and cover apples with brown sugar mixture.

Bake about 30 minutes at 375 degrees, serve with
a dollop of fresh whipped cream topping. made as
follows:

To 1 PINT WHIPPING CREAM, add 1 teaspoon VANILLA,
¼ teaspoon CINNAMON, and whip until peaks begin to
form. Serve on either warm or cool apple crisp.

A favorite dessert from childhood to the present.

Quoting my mother, "you'll have to use your own
judgment, but don't forget--the men I cooked for
worked long hours in fresh air, so thought everything I cooked was great."

Stan Lynde

---

*Stan Lynde is best known for a nationally syndicated comic strip that he created in 1958. He brought Rick O'Shay and
his gunslinger pal, Hipshot Percussion, into the hearts of people for 19 years. An original "Rick" drawing hangs in the
Louvre in Paris. A native of Lodge Grass, Lynde now lives in Whitefish.*

McGuane Ranch
McLeod, Montana 59052

My daughter Anne and I are enthusiastic spectators of Laurie's highly developed cooking skills. This recipe is high on our list of requests. It is, however, a poor choice for dieters because of its effects on restraint.

ANNE'S FAVORITE PORK ROAST

2 pounds boneless pork loin
3 tablespoons butter
2 tablespoons olive oil
1 teaspoon ground bay leaves
1 tablespoon whole peppercorns
Salt
1 cup vinegar
1 cup chicken broth

Brown pork in butter and oil in heavy pot just large enough to contain meat.

When meat is brown, salt it on all sides. Add peppercorns, ground bay leaves, vinegar and broth.

Cook on low heat at least 2 hours or until meat is tender. If liquid evaporates, add more broth and vinegar.

Strain peppercorns from sauce. Arrange sliced meat on platter and pour sauce over meat.

Angus Cattle — Quarter Horses

Tom McGuane wrote the screenplays for Rancho Deluxe *and* The Missouri Breaks. *He and his wife, Laurie, and daughter, Anne, have a ranch near McLeod. His novels include* 92 in the Shade, The Sporting Club *and* Keep the Change. *He is on the Board of Directors for American Rivers, Montana Land Reliance and the Craighead Wildlife Foundation.*

SHRIMP & SAUSAGE KABOBS

1 red pepper, cut into 1 inch chunks

1 red onion, cut into 1 inch chunks

1 green bell pepper, cut into 1 inch chunks

1 lb. sausage , cut into ½ inch thick rounds

1 lb. large shrimp with tails peeled and deveined

Mustard Butter

1 cup unsalted butter
2 Tbls. minced garlic
3 Tbls. coarse grained mustard
2 tsps. worcestershire sauce
1 tsp. hot pepper sauce
1/3 cup lemon juice
salt & pepper to taste

Place vegetables/sausage and shrimp
on seperate skewers and brush generously with the
Mustard Butter. Place on grill and cook for 2
to 3 minutes on each side. Cooking time will
be longer for the vegetables and sausage
combination.

Serve with remaining
Mustard Butter as a dip.

Dave McNally

Dave McNally, a former pitcher for the Baltimore Orioles, was a four-time 20-game winner and the only pitcher to hit a grand slam home run in a World Series game. Dave and his family live in his home town of Billings, where he owns a car dealership.

SUMPN' SURE SMELLS GOOD AROUND HERE!

CHICKEN WITH ELK PEPPERONI
OR SOMETHING ELSE

This dish will profit immeasurably from the use of decent chicken. In our neck of the woods, we get superb fresh junk-free chicken from the Hutterites of Springdale--they come to town once a week and sell things from a truck. We can also get Hutterite chicken, albeit frozen, at John's IGA in Livingston.

The Something Else could be ham, sausage, even bacon, but you can't beat elk or other game sausage.

Sauté a quarter of a pound or so of pepperoni in plenty of good green olive oil, along with a whole head's-worth of peeled garlic cloves, till the sausage is nicely browned. Don't let the garlic burn or the whole dish will be bitter.

Remove the sausage and garlic and keep it warm. Cut up the chicken (I like to cut the pieces pretty small so there's a higher surface-to-volume ratio), and flour it lightly. In the same pan and same good grease in which you cooked the other stuff, sauté the chicken over medium-high heat till it's almost cooked. Add the sausage and garlic along with quite a bit of sage (fresh is best, your own dried is second best) and a few red pepper flakes. At this point I usually pour out most of the fat.

Add a half-cup or so of white wine and cook it down to a glaze over maximum heat.

Eat!

I like to serve this chicken with some slightly bitter greens-- escarole or Swiss chard--and mashed potatoes. The garlic, by the end, is sweet and soft, and it's mighty good smeared on chewy bread.

My wine preference would be a young, slightly acidic red--Beaujolais, Dolcetto, Cigare Volant--but almost any wine works with this dish.

> Tom McNamee
> West Boulder Ranch
> McLeod

Tom McNamee is the author of three books, The Grizzly Bear, Nature First: Keeping Our Wild Places and Wild Creatures Wild, *and* A Story of Deep Delight. *He has served as president of the board of directors of the Greater Yellowstone Coalition. He has a ranch on the Boulder River near McLeod.*

Wallace D. McRae
Rocker Six Cattle Co.

Wally asked me to send you one of his favorite recipes for your cookbook. He isn't a dessert eater but this is one he never turns down.

Old-Fashioned Bread Pudding

Place 4 cups soft bread cubes in buttered casserole dish.

Blend:

2 c. milk, scalded with 1/4 c. butter or margarine
1/2 c. sugar (white)
2 eggs, slightly beaten
1/4 t. salt
3/4 to 1 t. cinnamon OR nutmeg
1/2 c. raisins

Add to bread cubes in casserole. Place baking dish in pan of hot water 1" deep.

Bake at 350° for 1 hour or until silver knife inserted in center comes out clean.

Serve warm with or without cream.

Amount: 6 servings. Does not double well; make 2 casseroles instead.

Wally McRae, a third-generation Montana rancher from Forsyth and graduate of MSU, has had four books of cowboy poetry published. In 1990 he was the first cowboy poet and first Montanan to receive the prestigious National Heritage Award. Wally is a regular performer on the syndicated television program The West.

Maureen & Mike Mansfield

MOCHA-MACAROON PIE
(Served for dessert at the U.S. Embassy, Tokyo)

1 1/4 cups graham cracker crumbs
6 oz. (equals 1 1/3 bars) German sweet chocolate
2/3 cups chopped pecans
1 cup sugar
1 teaspoon baking powder
dash of salt
5 egg whites
2 teaspoons vanilla extract
1/2 teaspoon water
2 teaspoons instant coffee
1 cup heavy cream
1/4 cup confectioner's sugar

1. Crush crackers to make crumbs (can be as large as a dime).

2. Grate chocolate, reserving 2 teaspoons to sprinkle on top.

3. Butter 10-inch pie pan thoroughly.

4. Heat oven at 350 degrees.

5. Mix sugar with baking powder.

6. Beat egg whites (with salt) in large electric mixer bowl until soft peaks form.

7. Add sugar gradually, beating constantly. Continue to beat for several minutes after all sugar is added.

8. In another bowl, mix cracker crumbs, grated chocolate, nuts, and 1 teaspoon of vanilla extract.

9. Fold this mixture into egg whites without stirring very much.

10. Pour this mixture into pie pan and bake 30 to 35 minutes. (Edges should be just beginning to brown). Cool thoroughly for one or two hours.

11. About one hour before serving, add water to remaining one teaspoon of vanilla, add instant coffee and stir to dissolve. Add confectioner's sugar. Whip cream until stiff, add coffee mixture, spread over pie, and sprinkle reserved grated chocolate over cream.

Maureen and Mike Mansfield

Mike and Maureen Mansfield represented the U.S. in Tokyo while Mike served as Ambassador to Japan from 1977 to 1989. He was a member of the U.S. House of Representatives (1943-1953) and a U.S. Senator (1953-1977), and was Senate Majority Leader (1961-1977). He is Montana's most loved and one of the nation's most respected politicians.

SHELLEY BIRD MATTHEWS

Del Bonita Star Route
Cut Bank, Montana 59427

Christmas has always been my favorite time of the year. It's the only time I feel you can eat all you want of sweets like fudge, divinity, cookies, etc....And believe me, I hear no complaints from my family.

I never liked fruitcake, though, until I moved to Homer, Alaska in 1983. My mother-in-law was baking and sending goodies out for Christmas when I commented on how I didn't like fruitcake. She said, "Wait 'til you try mine." I did, and it was delicious. Whether you like or dislike fruitcake, I'm sure you'll love this recipe.

MOTHER-IN-LAW'S FRUIT CAKE

1 lb. butter
1 lb. powdered sugar
8 eggs, separated
2 oz. citron
2 oz. candied orange peel
1 lb. white raisins
1 lb. chopped pecans
½ lb. candied pineapple
3 cups flour
½ c. apricot juice

Cut up all fruit and soak in juice overnight. Cream butter and powdered sugar. Then add beaten egg yolks.

Add sifted flour, fruit and nuts. Fold in beaten egg whites (stiff egg whites).
Bake at 275° for 2½ hours but be sure to check periodically.

Shelley Bird Matthews

Shelley Bird Matthews was the first Miss Indian Rodeo America, the 1990 World Champion Barrel Racer at the Indian National Finals and, in 1991, she qualified for the National Finals Rodeo in barrel racing. Shelley lives and trains in Cut Bank.

MISSION MOUNTAIN WINERY

U.S. Highway 93, Box 185 • Dayton, MT 59914 • (406) 849-5524
Open May 1 thru October 31 for tours and tasting 10 a.m. to 5 p.m. daily

Mission Mountain Winery
Chocolate Dipped Johannisburg Riesling Shortbread

The Mission Mountain Winery was established in 1984 on the west shore of the Flathead lake. The first wine variety we produced was Johannisburg Riesling. This variety has won many national and international awards for us over the years. Wine has always been used in cooking and as a beverage with meals. This particular recipe is a favorite of all Riesling and cookie lovers. It was created by Tom Campbell, our winemaker (and cookie monster) to celebrate the harvest. Tom believes that the cook must sample the ingredients as well as the results, as is evident in the recipe.

3 ½ c. all-purpose flour
1 t. baking powder
½ t. salt
1½ c. softened butter
⅔ c. granulated sugar
3 t. Mission Mountain Winery Johannisburg Riesling
2 c. flaked coconut
12 oz. semisweet chocolate, melted with 1 T. vegetable oil
1 bottle Mission Mountain Winery Johannisburg Riesling
and wine glasses for cook and cook's helpers

Open the bottle of Mission Mountain Winery Johannisburg Riesling and pour the cook and cook's helpers a half glass. Enjoy a sip now and then while cooking, but always remember: moderation in all things.
Combine flour, baking powder, and salt in bowl and set aside.
In another bowl, beat sugar, butter, Mission Mountain Winery Johannisburg Riesling and stir until smooth and light. Slowly add flour mixture until all blended. Next, stir in the coconut. Form dough in 8" x 7" rectangle and freeze until firm—not rock hard.
Preheat oven to 300° F. Grease 4 large cookie sheets. On a floured surface, roll dough out to 16" x 14", about 1/4" thick. Using a floured knife, cut into 48 squares and arrange on cookie sheet. Bake for 25 to 30 minutes, until golden. Cool on racks.
Place melted chocolate mixture in small, deep bowl. Dip shortbread halfway in, then place on waxed paper on cookie sheets. Place in refrigerator to cool and set the chocolate. *Do not get moisture in the chocolate or it will clump!*
Serve with a glass of Mission Mountain Winery Johannisburg Riesling.

Mission Mountain Winery is a family-owned business, located on the west shore of Flathead Lake in Dayton. The vineyard was started in 1979 and released its first vintage in 1984. The wines of Tom Campbell, Jr., have met with excellent reviews, and have received international recognition and awards.

THE MONTANA BAND

When the Band came "off the road" after weeks away, I'd frequently get a phone call from Terry saying, "Get the meat loaf ready, Mom." And for someone who likes a recipe to follow, I've had a little problem putting this family favorite on paper. Ah well, here goes:

        2 lbs. lean ground beef
        1 cup (or so) fine bread crumbs
        1 egg
        1 package Lipton onion soup mix
        ½ cup bottled chili sauce

Mix together well, shape into loaf. Put 1 or 2 strips lean bacon over top. Bake 1 hour.   325° - 350°.

Nancy Hanna Robinson

The Montana Band started in the 1960s in Missoula as the Mission Mountain Wood Band. They played their way into the hearts of people with country blue grass, down home, get happy, dancin' music. In 1987, a plane crash ended their promising careers. Leader Terry Robinson's mom, Nancy, has shared Terry's favorite meatloaf recipe with us.

MILES CITY, MONTANA

THE PEACEMAKER
(For Company You Hate)

FRENCH BREAD	Cut almost through, more towards the top - then hollow.
GARLIC	Cloves of garlic, crushed and rubbed inside hollowed french bread.
BACON	Fry 8 to 12 strips of bacon - with butter added, set aside.
OYSTERS	A large wine glass (12 oz) or two of Oysters - slightly floured, salt and pepper, then fry for a short time in bacon/butter drippings remaining from frying bacon, set aside.
TOMATOES	Slice tomatoes, fry in remaining bacon, butter and oyster drippings, turn, lightly salt and pepper to taste.
COMBINE	Paint inside of bread with melted butter. Place oysters in bottom of loaf and cover with the crisp bacon. Place tomato slices on top of bacon. Close and wrap in aluminum foil.
BAKE	At 350° (preheated oven) for 20-25 minutes.
SLICE	With sharp knife, slice at angle or perpendicular.
SERVE	With mixture of mayonnaise with horseradish. Garnish with parsley and chunks of lemon.
BEVERAGE	Chardonay wine for zest.

Actually, we serve the Peacemaker to company we love, as well. The dish always evokes compliments and calls for more. One of our favorite recipes for one of the most valuable and oldest organizations in Montana.

Terry and Deborah Hanson

The Montana Bar in Miles City was established after 1890 in a marble-floored building dating from 1886. The bar has been restored and is perhaps the finest example of turn-of-the-century elegance found in Montana today. Over the past century, many a cattle, sheep, or horse deal was parlayed there.

Montana
Coffee Traders

We Roast Coffee

5810 Highway 93 S - Whitefish, MT 59937 - 406 862 7633 - fax 406 862 0074

Iced Cappuccino:

Dark roasted coffee
8-10 ounces Half & Half
1/2 cup sugar
Ice cubes

Brew a double strength large bistro of coffee.
Add 1/2 cup sugar to the hot coffee (or sweeten to taste), and pour into a pitcher and allow to cool for several hours in the refrigerator.
When cool, add the Half & Half to the coffee and stir. Pour over ice cubes in a tall glass and garnish with whipped cream and chocolate sprinkles.

Variations:

Add cocoa mix, chocolate syrup or chocolate milk to hot coffee.
Add 1 to 1-1/2 cups of malted milk powder to hot coffee mix, stir and cool. To serve pour over ice cubes in a blender and blend to produce a frothy head on the drink.
Add cooled coffee mixture to frozen banana(s) in a blender, blend with milk or chocolate milk for a coffee smoothee.

Coffee Coconut Cream Pie

1/3 cup flour	3 egg yolks
1/2 cup sugar	2 Tablespoons butter or margarine
1/8 teaspoon salt	1 teaspoon vanilla
1 cup strong coffee	1-1/2 cups shredded coconut
1 cup evaporated milk	Coffee Coconut Shell (see recipe below)

Combine flour, sugar and salt in top of double boiler. Add coffee and evaporated milk gradually. Blend a little hot mixture into lightly beaten egg yolks and return to double boiler. Cook 2 minutes, stirring constantly. Remove from heat. Add butter, vanilla and 1 cup coconut. Cool. Pour in Coffee Coconut Shell. Garnish with whipped cream and remaining 1/2 cup coconut, toasted.

Coffee Coconut Shell

2 cups shredded coconut	2 Tablespoons butter or margarine
Strong hot coffee	

Put coconut in a mixing bowl and add enough hot coffee to barely cover.
Let stand 5 minutes, then drain. Pat dry between paper towels. Rub butter on sides and bottom of 9-inch pie pan and press coconut into it. Bake in 350 degree oven for 10 minutes. Cool.

In 1982, R.C. Beall decided to bring great-tasting coffee to the state of Montana. He selects only the highest-quality arabica coffees from around the world, ships them to Whitefish, and carefully roasts them there. The coffee is distributed all over the U.S. and Canada. R.C. is now opening a roasting facility in Moscow, Russia.

—— 120 ——

Montana Governor's Cup Walleye Tournament

CHAMBER OF COMMERCE & AGRICULTURE, INC.

Glasgow AREA

BOX 832   GLASGOW, MONTANA 59230

TELEPHONE (406) 228-2222

Sams Supper Club
Friday Night Special
Stuffed Walleye with Seafood Sauce
Serves 6

6 Lg. (8-10 oz.) Walleye Fillets.

DRESSING

1 Bag Bread Cubes
1 Egg (whipped)
1 ½ tsp. Dill Weed
1 ½ tsp. Lemon & Herb Seasoning
1 tsp. Sage
2 C. Chopped Onion
2 C. Chopped Celery - Saute in 1 lb. of butter (Onion & Celery).

Add together in large bowl, moisten with warm water until consistency is firm.

SEAFOOD SAUCE

Melt 1 C. butter or margarine, add 3/4 C. of flour, simmer for 1 minute
(stirring constantly). Add 2 C. milk, stir until mixture thickens (on med. heat).
Add 1 can of small shrimp (drained), 1 C. crab, 1 tsp. lemon & herb seasoning,
½ tsp. dill weed, 2 TBLSP. of white wine, salt and peper to taste.

Skin Walleye fillet (it's easier to work with frozen fish). Cut fillet in half,
place fat piece on bottom of greased casserole dish, add dressing, top with
tail piece of fish fillet. Bake for 20 minutes at 400°.

Pour Seafood sauce over baked fillet. Garnish with fresh lemon and parsley.

ENJOY!!!

This recipe came about through peoples interest in Fort Peck Lake and craving
for Walleye. Not only is this the Walleye fisherman's favorite, it is also
Northeast Montana's favorite year round.

---

*Montana Governor's Cup Walleye Tournament is a major event that takes place on the the Fort Peck Reservoir. It draws
amateur and professional fishermen from all over the United States and Canada. The tournament is scheduled the third
weekend of July, each year.*

SAN FRANCISCO 49ERS

SUPER BOWL CHAMPIONS
XVI, XIX, XXIII, XXIV

Administrative Office

Marie P. DeBartolo Sports Centre

4949 Centennial Boulevard

Santa Clara, California 95054-1229

Telephone 408/ 562-4949

Fax 408/ 727-4937

JOE MONTANA'S . . . . <u>VEAL PICCATA</u>

<u>Ingredients</u>

1 pound veal scallops, pounded thin

Flour

Salt

Freshly ground pepper

3 tablespoons olive oil

1 clove garlic, minced

1/2 cup dry white wine

1/2 cup chicken broth

3 tablespoons capers

1 small lemon, peeled with all white removed, seeded and diced

2 tablespoons butter

2 tablespoons fresh parsley, chopped

- Flour veal. Season with salt and pepper.
- Sauté in oil until lightly browned, about 2-3 minutes. Remove from pan and keep warm.
- Add garlic and sauté briefly.
- Add wine and chicken stock and bring to a boil. Reduce to 1/3 cup.
- Stir in capers and lemon. Return to a boil.
- Swirl in butter and parsley, and continue cooking until sauce thickens and turns creamy.
- Dip veal slices in sauce to coat. Arrange on a platter and spoon the remaining sauce over the scallops.
- Serves 4

Joe Montana is a celebrated quarterback for the San Francisco 49ers, and has played in four Super Bowl Games won by the 49ers. With a name like his, we just had to have him in the book.

Montana Logging and Ballet Company

RECESSION TROUT
Which we can't afford at the
MONTANA LOGGING AND BALLET COMPANY
nor can you...

*This is an extremely tasty but rather expensive dish that many of us can't afford any more.

You'll need 4 Montana trout--rainbow, brown, lake, or cutthroat. If the recession has left you unscathed, hire some out-of-work person to catch them for you. If you have to ask, "Recession, what recession?", then fly them in from Seattle where they took them fresh off the plane from Missoula. If the recession did "scathe" you, catch the fish yourself, cook them up without the stuffing, invite over a couple of friends, and just look at pictures of crab, shrimp, and scallops.

4 medium-sized trout	1/2 teaspoon marjoram
1/3 lb. scallops	1 TBSP. chopped chives
1/3 lb. shrimp	2 TBSP. cooking sherry (dry)
1/3 lb. crab	1 clove minced garlic
1/4 cup bread crumbs	heavy cream
1/4 cup chopped toasted almonds	1/2 tsp. savory

Clean the fish, leaving head and tail on and the skin intact. Cut out the inside bones and meat of the fish, leaving 1/8" to 1/4" of the meat on the skin. If you're a Democrat, save the de-boned fish meat and add it to the stuffing. Tell your environmental friends you recycle. If you are a Republican, forget the recycling and get right to the expensive stuff.

Cut the de-boned meat into small chunks and mix with scallops, shrimp, and crab in a big bowl. Blend in bread crumbs, and add enough heavy cream to moisten.

Season with chopped chives, cooking sherry, minced garlic, savory, marjoram, and almonds. Actually the nuts are optional, unless it's national Politicians Week, when they are mandatory.

Stuff each fish with enough stuffing to fill the belly cavity and still allow the belly to close all the way. Cover with foil and bake at 375 degrees for 15 minutes. Then uncover and bake 10 minutes more or until the fish flakes easily. If you are a journalist, you may prefer the fish hard-boiled. If you are running for office, invite rich friends and charge them $500 per plate.

Enjoy!

Montana Logging and Ballet Company is a musical comedy group "dedicated to social justice, political satire, the Seattle Mariners and other lost causes...." In appearances across the nation, the MLBC uses humor and current political news to entertain and enlighten their audiences. Members are from Helena and Bigfork.

MONTANA
M A G A Z I N E

BOX 5630   •   HELENA, MT 59604   •   TELEPHONE 406/443-2842

I am <u>not</u> a cook, do not claim to be a cook and will probably never be mistaken for a cook. Although some do say I have the figure for it.

In enticing my wife to marry me, a promise was given that she would never have to cook on our backpacking trips. I would handle it all . . . After the first trip on which I lovingly prepared and served her various freeze dried dishes straight from the package . . . I no longer do the cooking. However, I can produce this wonderful recipe if called upon to do so.

Rick's Mushroom and Onion Bread

1 loaf French bread
a lot of mushrooms - sliced
an onion or two - chopped
garlic salt
butter or margarine
fake swiss cheese (processed)

Measuring only frustrates and confuses me . . . so there are no specific amounts of ingredients listed. All is done to taste and in whatever amounts seem appropriate.

1. Saute' lots of mushrooms and onions in a generous amount of garlic butter till mushrooms are limp and onion is transparent.

2. Slice a loaf of french bread in 1" slices, but don't cut all the way through.

3. Insert 1/2 slice cheese and 1 large spoonful of mushrooms, garlic butter & onion mixture in each cut. Wrap loaf in foil and heat in 350 oven for 20 minutes or until cheese melts.

Serve to family or company, and when they give you praise, say, "Thanks, I got this recipe from my friend Rick Graetz".

Rick Graetz
Rick Graetz
CEO and Publisher

Montana Magazine, founded in 1970 in Helena, is one of the largest regional magazines in the country. It is published six times a year.

— 124 —

10326 Montana Lane, Agua Dulce, CA. 91350   805-268-1946

CHICKEN AND BROCCOLI CASSEROLE:

Bake 6 Chicken Breasts for 30 min. Then debone and cut into bite size pieces.

Cook 3 large pkgs. of Frozen Broccoli or 2 lbs. Fresh Broccoli. Cut into bite size pieces.

In a large 13x9 baking dish place Broccoli on the bottom and cover with chicken pieces.

In a separate bowl mix together 2 Cans of Cream of Chicken Soup (do not dilute).
$\frac{1}{2}$ Cup of Sour Cream
$\frac{1}{2}$ Cup of Mayonnaise
$\frac{1}{2}$ Cup of Grated Mild Cheddar Cheese.

Spread this mixture evenly over the top of Chicken and Broccoli. Then sprinkle with 1 small can of Durkee's Dried Onions and 2 cups of Grated Cheddar Cheese.

Bake at 350° for 20-30 min. or until hot and the cheese is completely melted.

This is an easy dish that can be made ahead of time. We have served it to a wide variety of guests at the ranch, on original Till Goodan dishes. You will remember the ranch dishes with the brands around the edge and the bucking horse center.

Sincerely,

Montie Montana

Montie Montana, a living legend from Wolf Point, is surely the world's best-known trick roper since Will Rogers. In 1989 he was inducted into the Rodeo Hall of Fame. He has ridden in every Tournament of Roses Parade since 1931.

MONTANA POWER COMPANY

ROBERT P. GANNON
PRESIDENT

German Crackers

°   2 cups of flour.

°   Beat one egg and add enough water to make the dough workable so it can be rolled out very thin.

°   Cut the dough into irregular, approximate 3" x 5" pieces with a pizza cutter.

°   Prick each cracker with a fork.

°   Quickly deep fry in hot cooking oil, turning once.

°   A deep, heavy skillet works best.

My mother was born in Germany and came with her family to the Chinook area in the late 20s. The family later moved to Kalispell. My mother and father married in Kalispell and then moved to Butte. My grandparents ultimately relocated to Polson in the early 40s where they operated a bee business for many years.

Every summer, my older brother and I would leave Butte the day after school finished to go to Polson - not to return until the day before school began. He and I, along with a couple of our cousins, would spend the summer in Polson "helping" our grandad with "the bees". How lucky could we get - - - - spending the summer around Flathead Lake!

During the long winter in Butte, we would build a huge appetite for my grandmother's tasty homemade noodle soup and German crackers. The older grandchildren, myself included, typically would feast on our favorite dish while listening attentively to our grandparents telling stories of how our immigrant family made it to and worked to remain in Montana.

Bob Gannon

Montana Power Company, headquartered in Butte, is the only Montana-based company listed on the New York Stock Exchange. Formed in 1912, it has grown into a diversified corporation with more than 30 subsidiary companies in utility and non-utility businesses. Today, it has the second-largest utility service area in the United States.

—— 126 ——

This recipe came from relatives in the Midwest. Good Italian that my wife is, she doubled the amount of marsala. The result is one of my favorite dishes that makes most restaurant versions taste bland!

CHICKEN WITH MARSALA

    4 whole chicken breasts
    4 oz. butter
    1/2 medium onion, sliced thin
    1/2 lb. mushrooms, sliced thin
    1 cup marsala
    1/4-1 cup water
    salt and pepper to taste

Skin and bone breasts and pound with flat side of meat tenderizer until very thin. Heat skillet and melt butter. Season chicken and cook until lightly browned on both sides. Remove chicken. Saute onion and mushrooms in drippings 3-5 minutes. Add 2-3 tablespoons of flour and blend well. Add marsala and as much water as necessary to make medium gravy. Return chicken and simmer about 10 minutes. Serve with buttered noodles.

Sincerely,

JACK McCORMICK
WARDEN

Montana State Prison near Deer Lodge came into service in 1979, replacing the 110-year-old territorial prison on the town's main street.

Office of the President

103 Montana Hall
Montana State University
Bozeman, Montana 59717

Telephone 406-994-2341
FAX   406-994-2893

This hot crab dip recipe has been a favorite of our family for many years. In fact, several years ago when Kathy's son was working as a chef in a local restaurant, he submitted it for their menu, and it became a favorite there also. It is so good that it often upstages the main course of the meal that follows.

HOT CRAB DIP

1 8 oz package cream cheese
1 tablespoon milk
2 6 1/2 oz cans flaked king crab
2 heaping tablespoons chopped yellow onion
2 tablespoons horseradish
salt and pepper to taste
1/2 package slivered almonds

Cream softened cream cheese and milk. Mix in all other ingredients except almonds. Sprinkle almonds on top. Bake at 375 degrees, 15 minutes or until heated through. Serve with crackers.

* * * * * * *

Fudge is simply a very good example of one of America's favorite sweet dishes. Having eaten several thousand varieties of fudge over the course of a lifetime, I can recommend this as the best of all of them.

THE BEST FUDGE

2 cups walnuts, chopped
2 pkgs Bakers semi-sweet chocolate chips (lge pkg)
1 cube butter
1 tsp vanilla
1 lge jar marshmallow cream
4 1/2 cups sugar
1 can evaporated milk (lge)

Mix sugar and milk together, boil 6 minutes. Add chips, vanilla, and marshmallow cream, mixing well. Add butter and walnuts. When butter is melted, put in buttered pan. Cool.

Erin Go Bragh!

Michael and Kathy Malone

Montana Wilderness Association

Earl Velk's Alpine Soliloquy

- 16 ounces spaghetti
- 3 tablespoons olive oil
- 2 cups Parmesan cheese
- 2 tablespoons dried parsley flakes
- 6 teaspoons ground basil
- fistful of garlic, minced on site
- water

Boil water, cook spaghetti, drain. Add oil, toss, add other ingredients, toss again. Serves four.

"To 'bee, or not to 'bee" ... was never the question for the fabled founder of the Professional Folf Association, Earl Velk. Nor was there ever any question about how Velk, now Chairman for Life of the P.F.A.'s Rules Committee, nourished himself for his countless victories in high-altitude wilderness folf tournaments. While the also-rans outsmarted and underfed themselves with the freeze-dried food of flatulence, Velk made the effort to carry a couple of extra ounces in his pack and prepare a real meal.

One summer afternoon, at 7,500 feet in the Badger-Two Medicine and on the eve of the Summer Solstice Open, a sow grizzly and two cubs invited themselves to supper. While the humorless mother chased us up some nearby whitebark pines, the cubs raced for Earl Velk's spaghetti. They loved the garlic and would have eaten the whole thing, and maybe us, too, but Velk drove them off by drilling the sow square on the noggin with a 165-grammer.

It was a 25-yard shot, and Velk made it while dangling from the top of a spindly tree! Put a 'bee in his hand, and that's the way he is.

This is a real meal for real athletes. It's got vitamins B, C, D, calcium, magnesium, potassium, phosphorescence, carbon, dilithium, iron, and plain old mettle. "Frisbees is just like rockets," Earl Velk always said. "You can't send either of 'em into space without good fuel."

Why "Soliloquy"? After eating it, Earl Velk always had time for a speech.

Bob Decker, Conservation Director

P.O. Box 635 • Helena, Montana 59624 •   (406) 443-7350

Wilderness Folf
Letting fly on the Rocky Mountain Front

Montana Wilderness Association was organized in 1958. The MWA's prime endeavor has been to vigorously defend recreation and wildlife in the forest planning process. It is a powerful protector of Montana's wildland heritage.

THE GEORGE MONTGOMERY FOUNDATION OF THE ARTS
A Calif. Nonoperating Private Foundation

BAKED MONTANA JACK

Rabbit, That Is.

ONE WHOLE CLEANED RABBIT

George Montgomery
ACTOR, ARTIST, COLLECTOR

6 or so carrots
6 or so medium sized potatoes
2 celery stems
1 green pepper
6 or so green onions with tops

Place the whole prepared jack on its back in a roasting pan with a 1/2 cup of water.

Bake at 275 to 300° for about 3/4 hour, then add diced carrots, celery, onions, and green pepper (in season), along with quartered potatoes in and around the Jack-- baking all for an additional hour at 300°. Season to taste.

The above recipe works very well with chicken, pheasant, duck, beef, pork, and lamb (Black or White).

Serves 4-6.

George Montgomery was born on a farm a few miles east of Brady and went to school in Manson, Ledger, Black Eagle, Great Falls and at the University of Montana. He became a successful Hollywood actor, director, producer and writer, and an art collector, sculptor, and furniture designer. He has a home near Lincoln.

Moose's Saloon is a classic old fashioned independent pizza and beer place. In addition to pizzas we serve soup and sandwiches. One of our most popular sandwiches is the "Missoulian". This sandwich originated when a group of Kalispell employees from the Missoula newspaper called the "Missoulian" liked our roast beef and swiss cheese sandwich but insisted that we put fresh mushrooms on the sandwich when we heated it in the oven. Within a year other people tried this sandwich and liked it so well, it became our best seller.

Ingredients:
3oz roast rare beef	mayonnaise
2 slices of swiss cheese	6" swiss boy style roll
handfull of fresh sliced mushrooms	

Method:
Slice bun, place the ingredients on the open faces, heat in the oven until the cheese is melted and the mushrooms are hot. Spread with mayonnaise and serve with a pickle and potato chips.

One of the nicest parts of being in business is when you are recognized by other people for something you do well. In this case it wasn't "Moose" Miller but Ruth Rose, our kitchen leader and soup cook who was singled out in 1986. In a national menu contest put on by the Whirl Golden Ladle Club, Ruth took third prize (a diamond watch) in the appetizers, snacks, and soups division. It is with pleasure that we offer her **Creamy Celery Zucchini Soup** recipe here.

Ingredients:
6 C sliced celery	2 sprigs parsley, snipped
6 sliced green onions	4 tbsp Whirl or butter
2 medium zucchini	3 heaping tbsp flour
2 heaping tbsp chicken stock or base	4 C half & half
	Salt & pepper to taste

Method:
- Cook celery, onions, zucchini, chicken base until tender; add salt.
- Make roux of Whirl or butter and flour, then add half & half.
- Pour into celery, onions, and zucchini, add pepper and serve with croutons.

My thirty-five years of running "Moose's" Saloon have been filled with many good times, many more great friends, and an unbelievably super staff. It is a lovely feeling when your people get to share the sunshine with you! Thank you very much for allowing us to be part of your cookbook and helping you in a very noble cause.

Your Friend "Moose"

Moose's Saloon, in the Flathead, has been a major attraction since the 1960s. Its hallmark has always been sawdust and peanut shells on the floor. It's a great place for lunch or pizza after the game. Moose Miller, owner and namesake, has long been tireless in his support of the Kalispell community and its young people.

BILLINGS
PRESERVATION
SOCIETY

APRICOT JAM

1 # fresh apricots to 1 # sugar

Wash apricots and peel. Put sugar over the fruit and let
it stand until the sugar melts. Place in kettle over a
slow fire and boil for two hours. Stir often. If it should
become too stiff before the fruit is cooked, add a little
water. Crack pits and place kernels in hot water, blanche
and add to fruit about 15 minutes before done.

ORANGE MARMALADE

9 oranges, sliced thin
3 grapefruit, peeled
6 lemons, sliced thin
2 pints of water to each pint of fruit

Let stand overnight. Next morning, boil down to half.
Measure again and add one pint sugar for each pint fruit
and juice. Cook until it jellies.

These recipes are from the Moss family recipe files. Hot
biscuits were a family favorite and legend claims they were
served with every meal. Although the Moss family had a
cook during P.B.'s lifetime, Mattie Moss and her daughter,
Melville, did have favorite recipes they like to prepare.
These would have been wonderful accompaniments to the
baking powder biscuits so popular with the family.

Ruth Towe
Ruth Towe, Director
The Moss Mansion

The Moss Mansion in Billings was built in 1903 for the Preston B. Moss family. This turn-of-the-century home, listed on the National Register of Historic Places, is open for tours.

MOUNTAIN SKY

GUEST RANCH

P.O. Box 1128, Bozeman, Montana, 59715 (406) 587-1244 1-800-548-3392

Steve Pedalino has been the head chef at Mountain Sky for the past ten years and guests have delighted in his House Salad. Many have asked for this recipe time and again. Steve has passed it on to me to share with all of you. Enjoy!

Alan Brutger

Vinton Salad ala Mountain Sky

3 bags or 3 bunches fresh spinach (washed and dried)
3 hard boiled eggs chopped
1/2 pound bacon chopped and cooked (saving a little bacon fat)

Dressing:
> 3 tablespoons mayonnaise
> 1 tablespoon dijon mustard
> 1/4 cup chopped onion
> 1/4 cup chopped parsley
> 1 tablespoon paprika
> 2 cloves garlic minced fine
> 1/2 teaspoon salt
> 1/2 teaspoon white pepper
> 1 teaspoon worchestershire
> a few drops of tabasco
> 1 egg
> 1/4 cup white vinegar
> 1 quart salad oil

For the dressing, put first 11 ingredients in electric mixing bowl or stainless steel or crockery bowl. Using wire whisk, mix all ingredients well - pour a bit of the vinegar in - then slowly add in the oil by a thin stream. Add remaining vinegar and adjust seasoning adding more salt and pepper to taste.

Put spinach, egg and bacon in separate mixing bowl - drizzle with a small amount of bacon fat. Pour a portion of the dressing over the salad (not all of the dressing). Toss well and serve on chilled plates.

Notes on Serving: Serve with a dry French or California Chardonnay or Italian Soave. This salad is wonderful as a starter for a veal, chicken or pork dish or serve a larger helping as a light meal with crusty bread and soup.

This recipe serves 12 persons.

Buon Appetito
Chef Pedalino ☺

Mountain Sky Guest Ranch, located in the beautiful Paradise Valley, has been catering to families since the 1930s. Horseback riding, blue-ribbon trout streams, outstanding scenery and excellent gourmet food lure vacationers to this mountain dude ranch.

Colin Murnion

NFR Bareback Rider

Whenever I pass by home I look forward to my dad's sour dough pancakes.

SOUR DOUGH PANCAKES

Starter:

Combine in crock or glass jar and let stand for 2 or 3 days until bubbly:

> 1 pkg. yeast
> ½ c. sugar
> ½ c. flour
> 1½ c. warm water

The night before add water and flour enough for your family, enough to make a thick sponge. Let stand until morning. Pour into bowl and leave about a cup of starter in jar.

Combine with starter in bowl:

> 1 t. salt
> 1 t. soda
> ½ c. sugar
> 2 eggs

Cook on hot griddle.

Colin Murnion is a four-time National Finals Rodeo qualifier, 1987-1990, and the 1986 and 1989 Montana Pro Rodeo Bareback Champion. He lives in Jordan.

Brent Musburger

I was raised in Montana during the steak and potatoes era. Like a lot of other people my eating habits have changed, and although I still eat beef, I don't eat it as often. One of my favorite alternatives is this recipe for shrimp boiled in beer. Hope you enjoy it.

INGREDIENTS:

2 POUNDS MEDIUM-SIZED SHRIMP
2 12-OUNCE BOTTLES OF BEER
1 CLOVE GARLIC, CRUSHED
2 TEASPOONS SALT
1/2 TEASPOON THYME
2 BAY LEAVES
1 TEASPOON CELERY SEED]
1 TABLESPOON PARSLEY, CHOPPED
1/8 TEASPOON CAYENNE PEPPER

FOR DIP:

MELTED BUTTER, LEMON JUICE AND HOT SAUCE;
OR LIGHT MAYONNAISE AND COGNAC

Wash the shrimp, but do not remove shells. Fill a large pot with cold water, bring to a boil and add all ingredients, shrimp last. Bring the water to a second boil, reduce heat and simmer, uncovered, for 2 to 5 minutes, until all shrimp are pink (DO NOT OVERCOOK). Drain and serve with melted butter seasoned with fresh lemon juice and hot sauce, or serve cold with light mayonnaise seasoned with a splash of cognac. Serves 4 to 6.

Brent Musburger

ABC SPORTS, 47 WEST 66 STREET, NY, NY 10023

Brent Musburger is a nationally televised sportscaster for ABC. He is a native of Billings and today owns a ranch north of Big Timber and property at Eagle Bend near Bigfork.

CHICKEN TORTILLA CASSEROLE

4 whole large chicken breasts
1 lb. Monterey Jack cheese, grated
12 corn tortillas, cut into eighths
1 can mushroom soup
1 can cream of chicken soup
1 can (small) green chile peppers, washed and chopped
1 small onion, chopped
1 small carton sour cream
1/2 cup milk
Salt and pepper

Cook chicken and cut meat into bite-sized pieces. Make sauce from soups, chile, peppers, onion, sour cream, milk, salt and pepper. Butter a long and narrow (3-quart) pyrex casserole and layer the bottom with 1/2 the tortillas, then 1/2 the chicken, 1/2 the sauce, 1/2 the cheese. Make another layer in this manner with the remaining ingredients, ending with the cheese. Make the day before and refrigerate. Bake before serving at 350 degrees for 45 minutes covered, and 15 minutes uncovered. Serves 8. (This can be frozen and baked after thawing.)

Judy Weaver

Judy Weaver

Rachael Myllymaki

Bran Muffins by the Pailful

Pour 2 cups boiling water over 2 cups All-Bran (100% Bran) cereal. Set aside to cool.

Cream together 1 cup Crisco oil or 1 cup margarine and 3 cups white sugar.

Add 4 cups bran flakes cereal, 1 cup natural bran and 1 quart buttermilk.

Add 5 cups flour,
3 T. baking soda,
1 T. salt.
Add 2 to 3 cups raisins and cooled all-bran.

Combine ingredients in order given. Mix batter in gallon ice cream pail. Store in refrigerator in covered pail and let stand one day before using. When ready to use, scrape batter off the top. *Do not stir* after storing.
Refrigerate remainder. Batter keeps six weeks and makes 6 dozen muffins!

Bake 20 minutes at 375°.

Rachael Myllymaki

Rachael Myllymaki is a champion barrel racer. In 1988 she became the youngest contestant ever to qualify for the National Finals Rodeo. In 1989 she was the National Dodge Circuit Champion. Rachael is an honor student at Arlee High School.

JIM NABORS

I've always enjoyed chili and since leaving Alabama years ago, I have tasted just about every version you can think of. And they have all been very good. But my favorite chili recipe is still the one that my mother and sisters used back in Alabama. I remember all of us sitting down to a dinner of chili and southern style cornbread. So not only do I find this chili my favorite, but eating it brings back fond memories of my family and Alabama. I hope you enjoy it, too.

JIM'S ALABAMA CHILI

1 lb ground beef
2T fat
1t salt
2 to 3 T chili powder
1 (8oz) can tomato sauce
1 (no. 2) can red kidney beans

1 medium size onion, finely chopped
2T vinegar
1/2 t garlic powder
1 large can tomatoes

Heat fat then quickly brown meat, stirring with a fork. Add remaining ingredients. Mix well, cover and simmer, stirring occasionally for 30 to 45 minutes.

Serves 4.

Jim Nabors is an actor and singer and is best known for his hit TV series Gomer Pyle, U.S.M.C. from 1964 to 1972, The Andy Griffith Show from 1963 to 1964 and the Jim Nabors Show. Jim has five gold albums. He owns a home outside Whitefish.

N.O.T.R.A.

PUMPKIN PIE

6 Eggs	Beat eggs slightly

1 - 29 oz can Solid Pack Pumpkin

2 cups Brown Sugar

2 teaspoons Cinnamon

1 teaspoon Allspice   Add all ingredients
except milk and blend
thoroughly and then add
the milk.

2 teaspoons Nutmeg

2 cups undiluted Canned Milk

Divided into 2 unbaked pie shells   Bake at 400 - 45 minutes

PIE CRUST

2 cups flour   2/3 cup shortening   3/4 teas. salt

Mix the above ingredients

1 egg, beaten and 1/4 cup water Mix well and add to the flour
mixture.   Will make two pies

This has always been a family favorite and for all special
occasions and holidays, I am expected to bring the pumpkin pies.

Gay Holliday

*The National Old Timers Rodeo Association is headquartered in Roundup. The Senior Pro Rodeo Tour promotes the
recreational aspects of rodeo competition. Two thousand members, all over the age of 40, compete in the
association's 60 rodeos each year throughout the U.S. and Canada.*

New Oriental Restaurant

3 Custer Avenue
Billings, Montana 59101

Beef Yaki Soba
(serves 4)

8 oz. chuka soba (Japanese-style noodles)
1/4 lbs. beef (shredded)
1/2 cabbage (shredded)
1/4 lbs. bean sprouts
1/2 carrot (shredded)
1/2 green pepper (shredded)
1 med. onion (sliced)
1/2 red pepper (shredded)
4 oz snow peas (whole)
1/2 lbs. mushrooms (sliced)
4 T. vegetable oil
2 T. soy sauce
1/2 t. salt
1/2 t. black pepper

Boil the soba in large pan about 5 minutes. Rinse and put aside.

Wash all the vegetables and drip dry.

Heat wok until very hot over high heat.

Add 2 T. of vegetable oil. When oil just begins to smoke, add beef and stir fry until golden brown, then add all the vegetables and stir fry about 1 minute. Do not overcook.

Add 2 T. vegetable oil and soba; stir fry (about 1 minute).

Pour in 2 T. soy sauce, 1/2 t. salt, 1/2 t. black pepper. Taste and adjust seasoning.

Serve immediately!!

The New Oriental Restaurant in Billings has been in business since 1989, and is owned and operated by Soon Joo and her daughters, Youn Park and Mi Sanderson. It is a small, cozy, family-type restaurant that specializes in authentic Korean and Japanese cuisine made from scratch.

BARBARA'S CHEESECAKE

Crust
1 1/2	cups graham cracker crumbs
2	tablespoons sugar
1	teaspoon flour
1/4	cup melted butter

Filling
2	pounds cream cheese, softened
1	cup sugar
2	eggs
2	teaspoons vanilla

Topping
1	pint sour cream
3/4	cup sugar
3/4	teaspoon vanilla
1/2	teaspoon lemon juice

Preheat oven to 350 degrees.

Combine all ingredients for crust in a medium mixing bowl. Press into a 10-inch springform pan. Bake for 5 minutes. Remove from oven and allow to cool. Turn off oven and open door to cool.

Mix all ingredients for filling in a bowl and pour into the cooled crust. Place in cold oven and turn to 350 degrees. Bake 1/2 hour.

Combine all topping ingredients and pour over baked cheesecake. Return to oven for 8 minutes longer. Chill overnight.

Serves 18-20.

Can't think of an anecdote...
but Jack loves cheesecake, and
this is his very favorite!!!

Barbara Nicklaus

Barbara Nicklaus has raised millions of dollars for charity through her personal involvement in golf-related events. In 1990 she received the prestigious Ambassador of Golf award.

Jack Nicklaus

GUACAMOLE DIP

```
2     avocados, peeled and pitted
1     medium onion, chopped
2     green chili peppers, chopped
1     tablespoon lemon juice
1     teaspoon salt
1/2   teaspoon coarse ground pepper
2     medium size tomatoes, peeled and finely chopped
      mayonnaise (1/4 to 1/2 cup)
      tortilla chips
```

Put avocados, onion, green chilies, lemon juice, salt and pepper in Cuisinart. Mix until creamy. Add mayonnaise. Mix.

Remove mixture from Cuisinart and add chopped tomatoes. Stir gently.

Cover and chill.

Serve with tortilla chips.

We have avocado trees in our yard, and this is one way we enjoy using them.

Jack Nicklaus is one of the greatest golfers of all time, many say the best. He has won every major golf championship, and more tournaments than any other pro. Also a highly successful golf course designer, he owns a hunting lodge in the Noxon area and another near Essex.

CROW TRIBAL COUNCIL

P.O. Box 159
Crow Agency, MT 59022

(406) 638-2601

CLARA NOMEE, Madame Chairman
JOSEPH PICKETT, Vice Chairman
BLAINE SMALL, Secretary
SYLVESTER GOES AHEAD, Vice Secretary

Crow Country

BERRY PUDDING 6 SERVINGS
Ingredients

***1 pint dried or frozen berries (preferably choke cherries, June berries, or service berries
***4 cups water
***8 tablespoons flour
***1.5 cups sugar

Preparation

Mix flour and water. Boil berries. Add flour/water mixture and boil additional 7 to 10 minutes under medium low heat, stirring occasionally to keep from burning. Add sugar to taste. Serve warm.

FRY BREAD, a favorite with Berry Pudding
Ingredients

***3 cups flour
***3 teaspoons baking powder
***1 teaspoon salt
   (thoroughly mix above 3)
***2 tablespoons honey
***1 1/2 cups water

Preparation

After thoroughly mixing first three ingredients, use fork to add honey and water. With hands, make mixture into round 2 - 2 1/2 inch balls, making sure mixture is soft. Flatten ball by hand or roller to desired thickness. Preheat 2 to 3 cups oil in fry pan; fry bread til golden brown color.

Clara White Hip Nomee
Clara White Hip Nomee

Clara White Hip Nomee, as Madame Chairman of the Crow Tribe, is the first woman to be elected to the position. Her goal is education for her people, particularly for the young. Childless herself, she has raised 13 children. Clara's Indian name is Corn Pretty Blanket and she lives at Crow Agency.

NORTHERN
MONTANA
C O L L E G E
President

The following recipe is our favorite "pheasant" dish. We have been preparing it for family and friends for the past twenty years.

Bill and Vicki Daehling

Extraordinary Pheasant

Bone 4 to 6 pheasants (depending on size) and cut meat into bite size pieces. Brown the pieces in skillet in shortening. Place the browned meat into a large baking dish with a small amount of water. Sprinkle 1/4 cup of chopped green onions over the meat and add one 8 oz. can of mushrooms (fresh mushrooms may be substituted). Cover the dish tightly and bake at 350 degrees for 45 minutes.

Sauce:
1 stick (1/2 cup) margarine
8 tablespoons flour
4 cups chicken broth
1/2 cup wine (rose' or white)

Melt the margarine and stir in the flour completely. Gradually add the liquids and stir until thickened. Pour the sauce over the pheasant pieces in the baking dish and continue baking at 350 degrees for approximately 2 hours. Serve with your favorite rice or potato dish.

Northern Montana College was founded in 1913 in Havre. The college is a statewide resource for technology education and economic development initiatives, and also functions as a cultural resource and continuing education center for north-central Montana.

Sir Scott's Oasis
Box 348 - 204-W-RR. ave So.
Manhattan, mt.
59741

Pickled Cauliflower

1 Case - (12 heads Raw Cauliflower

1 5 gal Plastic Bucket

Boil 1 gal Distilled White Vinegar

2 gallons Water

2 cups salt

Pour over vegtables & Refrigerate
at least 2 days. They Will last
for weeks.

Additions optional
Celery
Carrots
Cocktail onions
Dried Red Chili Peppers (2 per gal)

R. Scott Westphal

Sir Scott's Oasis in Manhattan is known for its high-quality, generously-portioned steak dinners at low prices. During the tourist season, this popular restaurant serves more than 2,000 meals a week—in a town of about 1100.

CARROLL O'CONNOR'S PLACE

SHRIMP COCONUT

24 medium-sized Shrimp   1 Cup Flour
1 lb. Dry Shredded Coconut   Milk
3 Eggs   Salt & Pepper to taste
              1 Quart Peanut Oil

Clean and de-vein shrimp, leaving tails. Mix eggs, flour and
enough milk to make a heavy dough. Add salt & pepper. Lay
Coconut out on a tray, dip shrimp into dough leaving tails clean,
then roll shrimp in coconut and shake off excess. The above can
be done in advance and refrigerated until ready to use later that
day.

ORANGE SAUCE

2 (8 oz) Jars Orange Marmalade   2 Tbsp. Horseradish
1/4 Cup Dry Sherry   Few drops Tabasco

Put Marmalade through blender, mix with Sherry, Horseradish and
Tabasco to make a spicy orange sauce

Just before serving, heat oil to 375 degrees, Fry Shrimp about
3-4 minutes until coconut is golden brown. Serve on a bed of Rice.
Garnish with orange slices and serve sauce on the side

              Serves 4

Carroll O'Connor is best known for his role as Archie Bunker in television's All in the Family. *O'Connor is also a writer and producer with an M.A. from the University of Montana. He received the Emmy Award for best actor in 1973, 1977, 1978 and 1979. He presently stars in the TV series* In the Heat of the Night.

Chief of The Blackfeet Nation

Earl Old Person, Chief

P.O. Box 486
Browning, Montana 59417
(406) 338-7521 or 338-7276

BANNOCK BREAD

6 Cups	Flour
3 tablespoons	Baking Powder
1½ teaspoons	Salt
2½ cups	Water

Heat oven to 350°. Stir together; flour, baking powder and salt. Gradually add water, (if dough is too dry add more water). Knead until dough is not sticky. Grease a large baking pan, spread dough in pan and bake 35 minutes.

Serve hot with chokecherry jelly and thin sliced fried potatoes, beef from a roast, sliced thin before cooking and then fried. Peppermint tea or coffee is usually served with this meal.

This is a traditional meal for our people.

Earl Old Person is one of the most highly respected and honored Indian leaders in the West. A full-blooded Piegan from Browning, he has devoted his life to promoting and protecting Indian rights and interests.

patagonia

Yvon Chouinard's Tsampa

Real tsampa is stone ground roasted barley that is put in Tibetan tea along with rancid butter. This other version has been my principle expedition food for 10 years. I eat it twice a day on expeditions and I never tire of it. I come back from these trips healthier than before I left.

1. You need 7-grain cereal or some other coarse-ground multi-grains.

2. Soak cereal/grains in cold water for 15 minutes. Drain and rinse and drain again.

3. Pour rinsed cereal/grains into a well-seasoned cast iron frying pan 1" deep.

4. Heat over medium heat. Stir constantly for approximately 20-30 minutes, until grains are dry and golden brown.

5. Store in plastic bags in a cool dry place.

Tips:
You can use it as a cereal, or as a "carbo-extender" in dry soup mixes, or like rice, it cooks in 5-10 minutes. The best is to add it to Knorr minestrone soup. Cook as per instructions on package, add slivers of jerky for complete protein, and parmesan cheese.

—Yvon Chouinard

Patagonia is an international manufacturer of high-quality functional outdoor wear, founded by Yvon Chouinard, a world-class mountain climber, adventurer, strong environmentalist, fly fishing nut and gourmet cook. Yvon serves on the boards of two Montana conservation organizations. Patagonia has a presence in Bozeman and Dillon.

Greg Patent

APRICOT DESSERT BARS

This recipe won me second prize in the Junior division of the 10th Pillsbury Bake-Off way back in 1958. Art Linkletter was the master of ceremonies, and at the awards luncheon, Ronald Reagan (then, just an actor) sat at our table. Guest of honor, Irene Dunne, helped Art Linkletter award the prizes. What an experience that was! As a teenager my idea of fun was to spend the day in the kitchen playing around with food. That feeling has never left me; in fact it has gotten stronger with the passing of years.

1 pound dried apricots
2 cups water
1 cup + 2 tablespoons sugar
2 cups sifted flour
1/2 teaspoon baking soda
1/2 teaspoon salt
3/4 cup unsalted butter
1 cup sugar
1 cup sweetened shredded coconut
1 cup chopped walnuts
Sweetened whipped cream

Put apricots and water in 3-quart saucepan and bring to boil over medium-high heat. Reduce heat to low, cover pan, and cook slowly, stirring occasionally, until fruit is tender, about 40 minutes. Turn into large strainer set over a bowl and let cool slightly. Reserve 1/4 cup of apricot juice.

Mash together (or use food processor) the drained apricots, 1 cup + 2 tablespoons sugar and the reserved 1/4 cup apricot juice. Return apricot mixture to saucepan and boil, stirring almost constantly, for 5 minutes. Set aside to cool to room temperature.

Sift together the flour, soda and salt and set aside. Cream butter. Gradually add 1 cup sugar, creaming well. Blend in the dry ingredients to form a crumb mixture. Stir in the coconut and walnuts.

Adjust oven rack to center position and preheat oven to 400 degrees. Press 2 1/2 cups of crumb mixture in bottom and half way up sides of greased 13 x 9 x 2-inch pan. Bake 10 minutes. Spread apricot mixture over hot crust. Sprinkle remaining crumb mixture on top and pat crumbs gently into place. Return to oven and bake until top is golden brown, another 20 to 25 minutes.

Cool and cut into large bars. If desired, serve with whipped cream.

Makes about 12 large servings.

Greg Patent

Greg Patent, a chef from Missoula, has had his own TV cooking show and has written cookbooks. As a teenager, he created this recipe, winning a trip to New York to prepare it for judges of the 10th annual Pillsbury Bake-off.

The Grizzly Bear Project

Growl (handwritten)

My daughter Laurel was born in the Deaconess Hospital in Great Falls, Montana. My son Colin was born in a house in the Lower Sonoran desert. Here's a recipe for each of them:

Montana Chimichurri for pickling Big Snowy Mountains' Fairy ring mushrooms (<u>Marasmius oreades</u>) and marinating road-killed wild turkey. You can also pour it over lamb, vegetables, or game as a sauce.

I like garlic but 2 will do (handwritten)

This chimichurri is made by crushing (four) heads of garlic, a cup of fresh oregano, salt, a small onion, juice of one lemon, a half cup of olive oil, four kinds of chile including jalapeno, wild chiletepin, and, if you can find it, Argentine Layco Aji molido red chile. Put this in a red wine bottle with a little wine left in the bottom and fill it up with Dessaux red-wine vinegar. If you keep adding vinegar, it will last for a month or two. This chimichurri overpowers the hell out of the mushroom (blanch them first) flavor but the results are worth it.

Lower Sonoran clam chowder: Made on the winter beaches of the Gulf of California or, in this case, the Pacific Coast of Central Baja. From my field notes: "The sun was setting and the tide dropping as I dug among the rocks and coarse sand with a screwdriver, digging peck-sized holes into the lower beach for cherrystone clams (actually a small <u>Tivela</u>). The little venus bivalves were so common I had an easy 2-gallon bucketful in half an hour. I rinsed the little cherrystones between two buckets then set them aside in a pail of clean sea water to give them time to purge more silt from their digestive system. By dusk the fire was roaring on the upper beach and I had a skillet going with a half stick of Mexican butter, three slices of diced, parboiled Mexican bacon, a large white onion and a head of garlic. I boiled three big potatoes in a backpacking kettle at the same time. When I could stick a fillet knife into the spuds, I removed them and drained all but an inch of water. I added (clams) to the brim and covered the steaming pot with the lid. As soon as the clams steamed open, I plucked them out, eventually adding more and repeating the process until I had a pile of steamers, scraped from their shells with a Swiss Army knife. I gradually added a can of milk, blending it into the sauteed garlic and onion, them added the diced potatoes, a small fistful of ground hot red chile, a half-cup of white wine, a tiny sprig of fresh dill, salt and pepper, and the juice of four limes––all the time stirring and keeping the temperature well below boiling to avoid the inevitable curdling of boiling acidic milk and butter, finally adding the clams and heated up the whole thing to just below a simmer until the diced potatoes were <u>al dente</u>. The dew was sopping so I built up the fire to keep the moisture at bay. I ate the chowder in front of a roaring blaze of driftwood with the din of Pacific surf shouting in my ears."

save the juices if you can and add it to the soup (handwritten)

* I prefer my chowder unthickened and without cream—allowing clams and their juices to dominate the flavor. (handwritten)

Doug Peacock (signature)

Doug Peacock is an environmentalist, author and adventurer. He is best known for his studies of grizzly bears at what he calls "the Grizzly Hilton" near Polebridge. Doug is the model for Ed Abbey's legendary "Hayduke" character in the novel The Monkey Wrench Gang.

RIBS OZARK

(Originated at Bourbon, Missouri)

Take a whole uncut side of #2 grade hog ribs. Remove excess
fat and sprinkle with garlic powder.
Cook slowly over hickory charcoal. Apply sauce with brush
each time ribs are turned,(about four or five times) cook
until well done. When half cooked, toss a couple handfuls
of soaked hickory chips on the coals.
When done, cut ribs apart and let set at room temperature
for 30 minutes.

Sauce: Take 10 ounces of top grade hickory smoke barbeque
       sauce (the dark kind)
       Add ½ thimble of liquid smoke,
       A lump of brown sugar about the size of an egg.
       Thin sauce with a couple ounces of beer

CAUTION!! When serving to guests, don't ever run out of
these ribs as you might encounter hostilities similar to
what Jesse James experienced when he visited Northfield,
Minnesota to see the "sights".

Jack Reiner

The Prairie Symphonette was organized in Scobey in 1978. This town of 1,200 people boasts a symphony orchestra of 30 to 35 members, many of whom must travel from other towns to participate. People in this northeastern Montana community take their music seriously.

GINGER BEEF & BROCCOLI

1 lb. flank steak sliced thin (sliced at an angle)
4 slices of ginger root
1 bunch broccoli sliced thin (bite size)
1¼ C chicken stock
¼ C sherry
¼ C soy sauce
4 T peanut oil
1 T Sugar
¼ C cornstarch water mixture
1 tsp. salt

Heat oil and salt in wok, add 1 slice ginger. Remove ginger then add
beef to hot oil. Stir fry beef until pink is gone. Add stock, soy,
sherry, sugar and remaining ginger root. When liquid is boiling,
add broccoli and cover for two minutes. Add cornstarch water mixture
and stir until sauce is thickened.

***

Rozene & Charley Pride

Charlie Pride is a country-western singer with dozens of hit records. He is recognized as one of the top 15 all-time world record sellers. Charley and his wife Rozene lived in East Helena and Great Falls during the 1960s. Baseball brought him to Montana and a music career lured him away.

Royal Teton Ranch

Box A, Corwin Springs, Montana 59021-0881   406/848-7381

My parents taught me how to cook German and Swiss dishes. This is a hearty soup for winter months after skiing and outdoor activities. Especially good for colds and flus. A Sunday night supper complete in itself.

MOTHER'S CHICKEN SOUP
Makes 12 Cups

Broth Ingredients   3 stalks of celery, including leaves
                      1/4 bunch of parsley
                      1 small onion, whole
                      1 pound of chicken

Prepare the broth, preferably the night before. Bring 2 quarts of water to a boil. Wash vegetables and chicken. Tie celery stalks and parsley with kitchen twine and add with the chicken and onion to the water. Simmer together for 1 hour. When the chicken is tender, strain the vegetables and chicken. Reserve both the chicken and the broth. Cool the broth in the refrigerator for 12 hours to congeal the fat.

Soup Ingredients   1 cup of celery, diced 1/2"
                      1 cup of carrots, chopped 1-1/2"
                      1 cup of chopped potatoes with skin
                      1/4 cup of chopped celery leaves
                      2 cups cooked rice
                      1/2 cup chopped parsley
                      Salt and pepper to taste

Once the broth has chilled, remove the top layer of fat with a spoon. Prepare the vegetables for the soup. Bone and skin the chicken and cut it into 1" pieces. Bring the broth to a boil.* Add the celery, celery leaves and carrots. Lower heat so that broth simmers. Cook 5 minutes, add the potatoes. Cook another 5 minutes, add the chicken and cooked rice. Cook together until the chicken is hot. Season to taste. Just before serving, stir in chopped parsley.

*For a nice change add your favorite meatballs to the broth; simmer til done and add the other ingredients.

Happy Eating,

Elizabeth Clare Prophet

Elizabeth Clare Prophet
President

Elizabeth Claire Prophet is the spiritual leader of the Church Universal and Triumphant, which has its headquarters at Corwin Springs in the Paradise Valley. She is known as "Guru Ma" by her students and followers.

Classic Image Enterprises

P.O. Box 807
Valley Center, CA 92082

HUNTERS STEW

2 lbs. BEEF, BUFFALO, VENISON OR ELK

3 MEDIUM POTATOES

2 MEDIUM CARROTS

1 LARGE ONION

1/2 HEAD CABBAGE

1 14 OZ. CAN STEWED TOMATOES

1/4 CUP SOY SAUCE, MIXED WITH A PINT OF BEER

1/2 tsp. SAGE

1/8 tsp. COURSE GROUND BLACK PEPPER

NO SALT IS NEEDED , BECAUSE OF THE MARINADE

CUT MEAT INTO 1 INCH CUBES. PLACE IN BOWL AND COVER WITH
THE BEER-SOY SAUCE. MARINATE OVERNIGHT. LET THE MEAT DRAIN
WHILE YOU ARE CUTTING THE POTATOES, CARROTS, AND ONIONS INTO
BITE-SIZE CUBES OR SLICES. CUT THE CABBAGE INTO SIX PIECES.
WHEN THE MEAT IS DRAINED, PLACE IN LARGE POT, ADD POTATOES,
ONIONS, CARROTS, CABBAGE AND 14 OZ. CAN OF STEWED TOMATOES.
ADD 4 CUPS OF WATER, AND THE SAGE AND GROUND BLACK PEPPER
FOR SEASONING. BRING TO A BOIL, THEN TURN DOWN THE HEAT AND
LET SIMMER FOR THREE HOURS.

THIS DISH SERVES FOUR HUNGERY HUNTERS, HIKERS, HORSEMEN,
FISHERMEN, OR CAMPERS ON A COLD DAY.

I FIND THAT THIS STEW TASTES BETTER WHEN IT IS WARMED
OVER. IN FACT I LIKE TO COOK IT, LET IT COOL, AND PUT
IT IN THE FREEZER, SO WHEN I GO CAMPING OR HUNTING, ALL
I HAVE TO DO IS WARM IT UP.

ENJOY!

STEVE REEVES

---

*Steve Reeves is a bodybuilder who won the Mr. America title in 1947, Mr. World in 1948, and Mr. Universe in 1950.
He went on to become a successful actor, writer and physical fitness and health promoter. Steve was born
in Glasgow, and today has a summer cabin on the Swan River near Bigfork.*

ALICE RITZMAN
10432 South 46th Street
Phoenix, Arizona 85044
(602) 893-9716

If you ever have a short time to prepare a menu, but want it to taste like a gourmet cooked it—try this recipe.

Chicken Montardé
(for 4)

Put a medium-size casserole dish in an oven and turn it to warm.

   1-1 1/2 sticks butter
   6-8 chicken breasts (boneless, skinless)
   2 small or 1 large container of whipping cream
   2 heaping T. Grey Poupon mustard
   1 lemon
   1 jar capers

Pound the chicken breasts flatter with the flat side of a meat tenderizer.
Brown the chicken on both sides in butter in a medium-hot frying pan; pepper to taste. As pieces are cooked, put them into the warm casserole dish and sprinkle some lemon juice over them. Keep adding butter to same pan, keeping browned drippings until all the chicken is cooked.
Mix the mustard with a small amount of cream until it mixes well, then add remainder of cream for a smooth blend. Add this to the meat drippings and let thicken over high heat. When it is the thickness of a medium gravy, drain the liquid from the capers and add them to the sauce.
Pour the sauce over the warm chicken and serve.

I usually serve this with couscous and a fresh steamed vegetable. I also serve it with a rich, buttery California Chardonnay.
Being a professional golfer, I can't spend hours in the kitchen, but this recipe tastes like I have.

Bon Appetit!

Alice Ritzman was born and raised in the Kalispell area. She attended Eastern Montana College in Billings and was the 1975 Montana State Women's Amateur Golf Champion. Alice joined the Ladies Pro Golf Association Tour in 1978 and is ranked 32nd on the career-money-winning list.

ROCKY MOUNTAIN ELK FOUNDATION

2291 W. Broadway
Missoula, MT 59802
P.O. Box 8249
Missoula, MT 59807-8249
(406) 523-4500
"F.O. FAX" (406) 523-4550
"G.O. FAX" (406) 523-4581

LEFTOVERS

Traditions are such fragile things. I have started many — October camps in the Missouri Breaks, special huckleberry patches on the Kootenai, best friends over at New Years — but these rituals have changed with time, shifted to different places with new pleasures and less tradition.

I need to find new, fuller traditions. Not anything that needs too much attention, mind you. Just something I can keep alive — like sourdough — with infrequent but regular use. I am seeking new traditions right now, and it is enjoyable, despite the discovery that they need to fit an older body and tighter schedule.

Many past traditions, ones I've mostly lost, began without plan. The early-spring family hike across warm ponderosa-pined slopes just seemed natural after a few years repeating. Lois' sourdough-huckleberry pancake breakfasts and elk stroganoff dinners became Montana to lots of eastern friends and relatives who found their way to our door on summer vacations. And after a dozen winters of splitting larch kindling, I now know it was more than a chore — one not easily replaced by morning thermostat-setting.

I am still upholding the fine Montana tradition of hunting elk, but no longer care so much about success; in fact, empty-handedness may soon enough become the tradition. Friends and family (including me), who love the taste of elk, will surely resist it, I suspect. But then, maybe there's a tradition in the making here. I'll let my younger hunting friends know of our needs — the successful ones will have leftovers from time to time, and I could even give them some Tupperware with our name on it. Or maybe I could trade them this great recipe Lois dreamed up some time ago for leftover elk.

SOURDOUGH ELK ROLL-UPS

Filling:	Dough:
½ cup minced onion	1 cup sourdough starter
2 cups or more diced elk roast	1 t. sugar
3 T butter or margarine	1 t. granulated yeast
1 can cream of mushroom soup	2 T lukewarm water
2 cups elk gravy (more or less depending on how much you have left over)	4 T shortening
	½ t. salt
	1 t. baking powder
	1¼ to 1½ cups flour

To make filling: Blend ½ cup cream of mushroom soup and at least 1 cup of the elk gravy. (Reserve rest of soup and gravy for sauce.) Stir in minced onion and diced elk roast. (Reserve the butter to be dotted on the filling after it is spread on the dough.)

To make dough: Measure sourdough starter into a large mixing bowl. Add sugar. Dissolve yeast in lukewarm water. Add to sourdough starter. Cut shortening into mixture of salt, baking powder and flour, until it resembles coarse cornmeal. Add to sourdough starter, stirring well with a fork. Turn dough out on a lightly floured board and knead gently, adding more flour if necessary. Roll dough out into a rectangle about 9x13". Spread filling on dough and dot with butter. Roll the dough up lengthwise, like a jelly roll. Slice roll into about 9 slices, 1½" thick. Place slices in greased 9" square pan, cut side down, and cover with a cloth. Set in a warm place free from drafts and let rise for 1 hour. Bake at 375° F for 30-35 minutes or until lightly browned. Serve hot with sauce.

To make sauce: Add milk to reserved elk gravy and reserved cream of mushroom soup. Heat to serving temperature. Serves a family of 4.

The mission of the Rocky Mountain Elk Foundation is to raise funds for the direct benefit of elk, other wildlife and their habitat. These funds are used for many "on the ground" projects, including habitat enhancement and acquisition, research, management and conservation education programs. Bugle *magazine and* Wapiti *newspaper are published by R.M.E.F.*

Although originally concocted for use with leg of lamb, the following recipe is at least as pleasing to the palate when leg of venison (deer, moose or elk) is the meat of choice. My favorite is white-tail.

> 1/2 cup Dijon Mustard
> 1 Tablespoon soy sauce
> 1 clove garlic, minced
> 1/2 inch slice ginger root, minced
> 1 teaspoon crushed dried rosemary
> 1/4 cup olive oil
> 6-8 lb. leg of venison

Pre-heat oven to 325 degrees. Combine mustard, soy, garlic, ginger, and rosemary. Slowly whisk in olive oil. Thoroughly coat the meat with the mixture and let sit for 2 to 3 hours. Roast on a rack in roasting pan for 1 hour and 45 minutes.

I've also used this recipe on a covered barbeque grill with great success. A meat thermometer can be of help when using the grill. In either case, the pan juices make a good sauce when serving.

Hope you enjoy it!

Mark Moreland

Rocky Mountain Log Homes, of Hamilton, is one of the leading log home manufacturers in Montana. Their homes sell as far away as Japan, and they are representative of the creative and high-quality log home industry in Montana.

MEL RUDER

P.O. BOX 1389

COLUMBIA FALLS. MT 59912

COFFEE FRUIT DROPS

Recipe was obtained from Roger Gowdey, Whitefish, brother-in-law of Mel and Ruth Ruder.   Retired from Burlington Northern, Roger is a wonderful cook. He is pleased to have a part in the worthy project of a cookbook to benefit Intermountain Children's Home.

2½ cups peeled, finely chopped McIntosh apples
1 cup less 2 tablespoons <u>strong</u> coffee
2 tbl golden rum
1 cup white sugar
½ cup butter
1 cup raisins
1 tsp cinnamon
½ tsp cloves

3/4 tsp nutmeg
1 tsp vanilla
2 cups sifted flour
1 tsp soda
¼ tsp salt
1 cup chopped walnuts

Cook apples, coffee, sugar, shortening, raisins and spices in sauce pan. Cook gently until apple is tender - <u>Cool</u>.

Add vanilla to mixture. Blend flour, soda and salt - stir in - Add nuts.

Drop by heaping teaspoons on ungreased baking sheet.

Bake 375 degrees for 12 minutes.

Quantity - 6 dozen.

The Hungry Horse News started in a $25 a month office space, using a desk bought for $2.50, a portable typewriter and old Speed Graphic camera. I paid $30 a month for a room in the old Bank of Columbia Falls building. My meals were inexpensive.

Sincerely,

Mel Ruder

Mel Ruder founded the Hungry Horse News *and edited the paper from 1946 to 1978. He won the Pulitzer Prize for general local reporting in 1965.*

C.M. RUSSELL MUSEUM
400–13th Street North / Great Falls, MT 59401
(406) 727-8787 / Fax (406) 727-2402

Chocolate Chip Lonesome Dove Bars

(Makes two dozen 2-inch bars)

Bottom ingredients:
　　　1/2 c. shortening or butter
　　　1/2 c. white sugar
　　　1/2 c. brown sugar
　　　2 beaten egg yolks
　　　1 t. vanilla
　　　1/4 t. salt
　　　1/4 t. soda
　　　1 T. water
　　　2 c. flour
　　　1 c. chopped pecans
　　　1 package chocolate chips

Cream shortening and sugar.
Add remaining ingredients (except chips & nuts) and blend.
Mix well, pat into bottom of 8" x 12" greased pan.
Press one package chocolate chips and 1 cup pecans into dough.

Meringue topping:
　　　2 egg whites
　　　1 c. brown sugar

Beat egg whites until stiff.
Mix beaten egg whites and brown sugar.
Spread over top of mixture.
Bake 25 to 30 minutes at 325°.
Allow to cool for 20 minutes.
Cut into squares or fingers.

Submitted to C.M. Russell Museum Cookbook
by Sally Kuppinger Johnson, Dallas, Texas.

The C.M. Russell Museum in Great Falls is home to the art and personal items of western artist Charles Marion Russell.
The complex contains the national historic sites of his home, built in 1900, and his original log cabin studio, with a
museum housing his works, a Browning firearms collection, and Curtis and Sharp photographic collections.

N'IMPORTE QUOI
N'IMPORTE QUAND
N'IMPORTE OU

SALSA FRESCA SANTA CRUZ

This is a great cool and hot recipe that I enjoy during my summers on the beach in Santa Cruz, Ca.

3 medium-ripe tomatoes (1 lb.), chopped
1/2 medium red onion, chopped
6 sprigs cilantro, chopped
4 jalapeno peppers, chopped
3 green onions, chopped
4 cloves garlic, chopped
1/4 cup red wine vinegar
1/4 cup olive oil
1/4 to 1/2 teaspoon cayenne pepper
1 teaspoon sea salt

Mix all ingredients and serve as a dip or over diced avocado on a bed of leaf lettuce. Will keep for 2 days in the refrigerator.

Yields: approx. 2 cups

ENJOY!!

Scot Schmidt started skiing when he was four years old in his home town of Helena. Today, as one of the world's top extreme skiers, he has appeared in more than 20 movies, and is featured in The Best of Scot, *a ski movie by Warren Miller. Scot also designs technical extreme skiwear for the North Face company.*

KATHY GRIZZARD SCHMOOK
Box 136
Pray, Mt. 59065

After my illustrious ex-husband had a leaking heart valve replaced with one made of pig tissue, two things happened: First, he entered every hog calling contest south of Atlanta; and secondly he developed a penchant for pork. I experimented with many recipes but the one below was his favorite (except for the Spam soup he so dearly loved). I call it PORKY'S REVENGE.

5 lb. pork tenderloin (deboned)

Marinade:
1 cup chicken stock
1 small bottle soy sauce
3 T sesame seeds
3 T brown sugar
2 cloves crushed garlic
1 chopped onion
1 t ginger

Simmer above ingredients 30 minutes and pour over uncooked pork to let marinate over night (unroll meat if it's tied). Pour marinade off and save. Roast pork at 350 for 45 minutes. Cook reserved marinade down until thick (about 30 min.). Slice pork thin and let cool; sauce should be poured over meat and served at room temperature. Can be served in sesame seed buns as sandwiches or meat can be sliced thicker and served with brown rice.

Kathy Grizzard Schmook is the author of From Debutante to Doublewide *and* Purely for Prophet, *co-authored with Moira Prophet Lewis. Her "illustrious ex-husband" is syndicated columnist Lewis Grizzard. Kathy lives in the Paradise Valley.*

TED SCHWINDEN
GOVERNOR
January 5, 1981 - January 1, 1989

SCHWINDEN STROGANOFF

OR

How to eat well on a slender budget

Back in the "good old days", just out of the army, newly married, and struggling to make ends meet in the student housing in Missoula, Jean and I found the perfect supper [we didn't eat dinner until we moved to Helena in 1969]. With Jean working at the hospital to subsidize the meager G I Bill allowance that paid my way to a college education, we needed an evening dish that could be prepared in advance, provide a welcome alternative to macaroni and cheese, and macaroni and hamburger with tomato sauce. And, it had to be inexpensive!

So, to provide two suppers for two, one supper for four, just follow these simple directions.

Catch a sale on round steak, trim if you're watching cholesterol, leave the fat if you are young and foolish. We bought four pounds and saved half for swiss steak...our Sunday treat. Dice one and a half to two pounds of the steak into cubes of about 3/4 inch [or larger if you take big bites] and place in the bottom of a roaster. Empty a full can of mushroom soup over the meat and dump in a package of dry onion soup. Kind of stir it around a little bit so you feel you've played a major part in the outcome.

Now, put the cover on the roaster, place it in the oven at 250 degrees and <u>leave it alone</u> for at least four hours. Leave the cover on and resist every urge to take a peek...what you smell is the onion.

When you get home, or the hunger pangs are too strong to ignore, cook some noodles or rice...your choice...take the roaster from the oven, ladle the meat gravy over the rice or noodles and enjoy. I like to pour on a bit of soy sauce on my second helping.

From our university days, through the years on the farm, to the years of retirement we retained our taste for stroganoff...our <u>second favorite</u> family meal to our special chili. And that recipe is tightly restricted to our family!

Ted Schwinden

Ted Schwinden was governor of the state of Montana from 1981 through 1987. Born in Wolf Point, he is the owner and operator of a grain farm in Roosevelt County. Ted and his wife, Jean, now live in Helena.

NBC NEWS

Red Velvet Cake

1½ c. sugar
2 oz. red food coloring
2 T. cocoa
1 c. buttermilk
2¼ c. flour
1 t. salt
1 t. baking soda
2 eggs
1 T. vinegar
½ c. shortening
1 t. vanilla

Cream shortening with sugar, add eggs and beat well. Make a paste of cocoa and food coloring, add to creamed mixture. Sift flour and salt twice. Add buttermilk alternately with flour to creamed mixture. Add vanilla. Put vinegar in deep bowl, add soda (it will foam). When blended, add to creamed cake batter. Do not beat cake, just blend well. Grease and flour two 9" cake pans; pour batter into pans and bake at 350° for 25-30 minutes.

Cream Cheese Icing

3 oz. cream cheese
1½ c. confectioner's sugar
1 t. vanilla

Cream all ingredients together until fluffy and smooth. Will frost 1 cake.

I wish you great success with the cookbook. Good luck with what I'm sure will be a winner!

Willard Scott

Willard Scott is a radio/TV personality, weather reporter and performer on the Today Show *and NBC radio. He is active in many charities and owns a home in Big Sky.*

PHONE
406-338-5425

Bob Scriver
SCULPTOR

GARBAGE BEANS
By Lorraine Scriver

1 lb hamburger	3/4 cup brown sugar
1 jar brown baked beans	1/3 cup catsup
1/2 onion, diced	1/4 tsp curry powder
1/2 green pepper, diced	1/4 tsp ginger powder
1 stalk celery, diced	1/4 tsp garlic powder
1 small can crushed pineapple	Tabasco to taste (optional)

Sauté meat, onions, green pepper and celery untill meat is no longer pink. Skim off excess grease. Put beans and meat mixture into casserole, add rest of ingredients and mix well. Bake in 350° oven for 45 minutes to an hour.
Serves 4.

"My Godfather had been a French chef in Paris and came to Canada to live during the depression. Jobs were scarce and he was lucky to be employed as camp cook for the Provincial Parks Dept. in B.C. He had a bit of a drinking problem and this recipe was due to a hangover.
He had opened a can of beans the day before and forgotten them, next day the beans were still there and he was sure to be fired if caught wasting food, so he decided to start throwing this and that together and came up with this recipe of which was in great demand by all the men in the camps."

This recipe is from my wife, Lorraine — I am no cook but can emphatically recommend this dish to anyone! I'll guarantee they will want "seconds"

Bob Scriver,
Sculptor

Bob Scriver is an award-winning sculptor whose artwork has been shown nationally and internationally. He is the author of The Blackfeet: Artists of the Northern Plains *and two other books. Bob's studio is in his home town of Browning.*

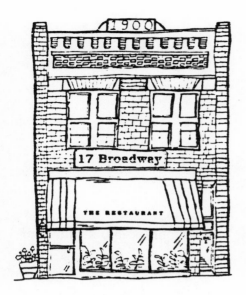

17 BROADWAY
THE RESTAURANT
Red Lodge, Montana 59068
446-1717

It is a pleasure to share the recipe for SPICY SESAME NOODLES with you. Pasta dishes seem to be a popular menu item in our restaurant, this one particularly because of its simplicity and unique oriental flavors.

17 BROADWAY'S SPICY SESAME NOODLES

8 ounces linguine
3 cloves garlic, minced
1 1/2 tablespoons brown sugar
4 tablespoons creamy peanut butter
1/8 cup soy sauce
6 tablespoons sesame oil
1/4 cup white wine
1/2 teaspoon crushed red pepper flakes
3 six ounce boneless, skinless chicken breasts (18 ounces), cut into thin strips
1 pound thin asparagus, trimmed, or other fresh green vegetables
        (pea pods or broccoli flowers)
3 scallions (green onions), white bulb and 3 inches of green, cut into 2-inch julienne.
1 small red bell pepper seeded and cut in 1/4 inch strips
1/4 pound mushrooms thinly sliced
4 tablespoons toasted sesame seeds

Bring a large pot of water to a boil. Add linguine, and cook at a rolling boil until tender. Drain, rinse under cold water and set aside in a large mixing bowl.
Place garlic, brown sugar, peanut butter, sesame oil, red pepper flakes and chicken in a large saute pan.
Cook over medium heat until cooked through. Add soy sauce and white wine and bring to a simmer. Cut asparagus on the diagonal into 1-inch lengths. Add asparagus, sliced mushrooms and red pepper strips to sauce and cook until tender. Toss noodles with chicken and vegetable mixture. Top with julienne scallions and toasted sesame seeds. Serve at room temperature. Serves 6.

---

17 Broadway is located in downtown Red Lodge. The building once housed a brothel upstairs and a meat market in the lower quarters. Today Sam Merrick and Bob Pitcher serve gourmet meals that create a balance between the tastes of local beef-loving folks and California herbivores.

DAVID SHANER
CLAYARTIST

7135 MONTANA 35
BIGFORK, MT 59911-6114
406-837-4388

CAESAR SALAD

LETTUCE: Wash 1 head Romaine. Dry well, break into mouth-size pieces. Refrigerate.

CODDLE EGG: Boil water and remove from heat. With a tablespoon, gently lower 1 egg into water. Remove after 6 minutes. Separate the yolk from the white.

DRESSING: Prepare in a large salad bowl.
      Mix: 3 medium clove garlic, crushed
      2 tbsp. Worcestershire sauce
      ½ tsp. dry mustard
      3 tbsp. anchovy paste or ½ can mashed anchovies
Add and mix well:
      1 coddled egg yolk
      1 tbsp. wine vinegar
      6 tbsp. olive oil
      Pepper

AT SERVING TIME: Place lettuce on top of dressing
Put "beaten until stiff" coddled egg white on top of lettuce
Gently toss egg white to coat lettuce, then deeper to include the dressing.
Add grated parmesan and croutons
TOSS, TOSS, TOSS.
Serve immediately.

The Best of Ceasar Salads!
It was served to me at the Frog Hollow Art Center, Frog Hollow, Vermont, and has become one of our favorites.

David and Ann Shaner

David Shaner, an internationally acclaimed, award-winning potter, has made his home in Bigfork for the past 20 years. He is best known for his use of earth colors and his simplicity of form.

Jimmy Shea
INSURANCE AGENCY

"Your Protection Is Our Profession"

•

Phone 723-6464

BUTTE, MONTANA

ROCK COOKIES

1 tsp. baking soda
3/4 cup hot water
1 cup brown sugar
1 cup shortening
3 eggs
2 1/2 cups regular oats
2 cups flour
3 tsp. baking powder
3 tsp. cinnamon
1 tsp. nutmeg
1/2 tsp. salt
2 cups raisins
1 1/2 cups walnuts

Dissolve soda in hot water. Set aside. Cream shortening and sugar until fluffy. Beat in eggs. Add soda water and dry ingredients and blend together. Add raisins and walnuts. Drop spoonfuls on cookie sheet. Bake at 375° for approximately 10-12 minutes.

Jimmy Shea

Walkerville, Mayor

Jimmy Shea was the mayor of Walkerville for 34 years. He also served as a state senator from 1971 through 1975. His success in public service can be credited to his credo: "All government rights belong to the people. Elected officials are not the government. They only serve as trustees of the people who elect them."

Brooke Shields & Company Inc.
Post Office Box B • Haworth, New Jersey 07641
Telephone (201) 385-9849

VEGETABLE HEALTH SOUP

2 medium Granny Smith apples, peeled and chopped

1 large onion, chopped

2 large sprinkles of Mrs. Dash

use any 1 of the following vegetables:

    1 large bunch of broccoli (do not throw stems away)

    1 large bunch of cauliflower

    1 large bunch of carrots

1 46oz. can of College Inn chicken broth (skim fat from top)

vegetable oil spray

Saute onions and apples sprinkled with Mrs. Dash in
    a teflon frying pan lightly sprayed with vegetable
    oil. Set aside.

Clean, scrub and chop the vegetable into 1" pieces.

Steam or parbroil vegetable.

Add all the ingredients to the chicken broth.

Cook 10 minutes.

Place all the ingredients in a blender. Puree.

May be served hot or cold with a dab of low-fat
    cottage cheese in center.

Garnish with parsley in winter, mint in summer.

Serves 5, approximately 125 calories in each serving.

Brooke Shields
xx

Brooke Shields is a highly accomplished actress-model, fitness enthusiast, business woman and writer. She graduated with honors from Princeton University. She starred in 14 films, including Pretty Baby, Blue Lagoon, Just You and Me Kid, Endless Love *and* Sahara. *Brooke has a home in the McLeod/Big Timber area.*

SIEBEN LIVE STOCK COMPANY

ESTABLISHED 1868

P.O. BOX 835
HELENA, MONTANA 59624

406-442-1803

FAX 406-449-8606

If it weren't for such a worthy cause this recipe would not be shared! I have used it for parties of 200, marinating in a plastic garbage can and stirring with a canoe paddle or pitchfork, and for as few as 6 or 8. It is _guaranteed_ to convert non-lamb eaters. This has been proven many times.

CHASE'S FAMOUS LAMB MARINADE

1 1/2 Cups salad oil
2-3 crushed garlic cloves
1 1/2 t. dried parsley
3/4 Cup soy sauce
1/4 Cup Worchestershire sauce
2 T. dry mustard
2 t. salt
2 t. pepper
1/3 Cup lemon juice
1/2 Cup red wine vinegar

Cut lamb (tender cuts, preferably legs) into lean, gristle-free 1" - 1 1/2" cubes. Marinate approximately 12 hours, turning occasionally. Barbecue cubes until pink centered. Guaranteed!

CHASE T. HIBBARD

Sieben Live Stock Company, located out of Cascade in the Big Belt Mountains, is one of the state's oldest and largest ranches. It is run by Henry Sieben's great-grandson Chase Hibbard, a fourth-generation Montanan.

This recipe is a favorite of mine both at home and traveling in Europe. It tastes so hearty and warm after training on the ice and doesn't take a lot of time to prepare.

CHEESE N' VEGETABLE SOUP

2 cups diced spuds
1½ cups chopped onion
1 cup sliced carrots
1 cup chopped celery
2 cups water
¼ cup butter or marg.
6 tsps. chicken instant bouillon
   or 6 chicken bouillon cubes

2 cups milk
½ cup flour
3 cups shredded Cheddar Cheese
1 tsp. dry mustard
1/8 tsp. cayenne pepper

In 4-qt. saucepan, combine spuds, onion, carrots, celery, water, butter & bouillon. Bring to a boil, reduce heat, cover and simmer 30 min. or until vegetables are tender.

In small bowl or blender combine milk & flour - beat until smooth. Gradually blend into vegetable mixture. Add cheese, mustard & pepper- cook & stir until cheese melts. (Makes 2 quarts or 6 servings)

*I've found out that you don't need as much cheese and you can add more milk if you want it to be more soupy. Sometimes I add sliced Polish Sausage. Enjoy on a cold winter day!

Dave Silk

David Silk is a Butte native and a 1984 Olympian. He won the 5,000 meter World Cup Speed Skating Championship in 1986.

6 3 SIXTY THREE RANCH

· Mission Creek Canyon · P. O. Box 979 · Livingston, MT. 59047 · (406) 222-0570

The 63 Ranch is happy to join in this very worthwhile cause to help the Intermountain Children's Home and share with the generous supporters one of our favorite recipes.

Cherry Pie is an old time western favorite and that reminds me of Red Burke, our Game Warden when I was growing up. It seems that cherry pie was "Reds" very favorite and Mother and I always tried to have one baked up when, we knew he might be visiting us, during his travels through the Montana mountains. For this you needed a round whiskey bottle to roll out dough and for "Red" to have a swig from, a can of pie cherries and fresh lard and flour for the crust.

First fire up the wood range, so the oven will be good and hot when you have the pie ready for the oven. Set out the granite pans and ingredients as follows;

Mix in a pan and cook over moderate heat, in the middle of the wood stove top, the following ingredients; 3/4 cup of sugar or 1 cup if the cherries are really sour, 4 tablespoons of flour; add 1/4 teaspoon almond flavoring, a few drops of red food coloring and 2 1/2 cups of canned pie cherries and juice. Stir well and constantly until the mixture thickens and boils.

Set aside while you make the crust:

Sift together, 2 cups all purpose flour with 1 teaspoon of salt, into a bowl. Add and cut in, with a pastry blender, 1/3 cup of lard till the size of meal, then add 1/3 more cup of lard and cut in until the size of peas. Add 4 tablespoons of crick water and mix just till blended with a fork. Smooth to a round ball and cut dough in half. Roll out each half, on a floured table top, until quite thin, with the whiskey bottle.

Line the pie pan with the first circle of dough that you have rolled out. Pour in the filling and dot with butter. Cut in strips about 1/2 inch wide the circle of dough that you have waiting. Weave a lattice top on the cherry pie. Fancy up the edge and pop in your wood burning cook stove oven which is hopefully up to 425 degrees by now and cook for 30-40 minutes.

Watch carefully, as cherry pies at high altitude tend to boil over and that is the reason for the lattice crust to let some of the steam off without boiling out of the pie.

Now you had better put the coffee pot on for "Red" might come riding in at any time and he'll be hungry as a bear.

MEMBER

DUDE RANCHERS
ASSOCIATION

Enjoy,

Sandra C. Cahill

A National Historic Site

The 63 Ranch is a dude ranch owned and operated by the Christensen family since 1929. Breathtaking scenery, great food and a "welcome to our home" atmosphere keep guests coming back year after year. It is located in the beautiful Absaroka Mountains near Livingston.

The Big Sky Country

MONTANA STATE SENATE

SENATOR ED B. SMITH

SENATE DISTRICT 10

  HELENA ADDRESS:
    CAPITOL STATION
    HELENA, MONTANA 59620
  HOME ADDRESS:
    DAGMAR, MONTANA 59219
    PHONE: (406) 483-5484

COMMITTEES:
  FINANCE & CLAIMS
  EDUCATION
  FISH, WILDLIFE & PARKS

The Smiths have always had a large garden dating back to the "Dirty Thirties" when you had to produce much of your own food if you wanted to eat through the long winters. After canning, storing and giving away many of our vegetables, we still had some left so Juliet said, "let's try salsa."

ED & JULIET'S SALSA

3 lbs. tomatos, peeled & chopped
1 large onion, chopped
2 green peppers, chopped
3 to 4 hot chili peppers, chopped (fresh or canned)
2 tsp. garlic powder
2 tbsp. vinegar

Simmer for 30 minutes. Put in hot jars. Seal. Process in hot water bath for 15 minutes.

Hints:
1. After chopping tomatos, drain off some of juice before cooking.
2. About 5 canned hot chilis with 1 tbsp. juice make a medium hot salsa.
3. About 6 to 8 chilis make a hot salsa.

This recipe was published in the Billings Gazette when Ed ran for Governor and many people told us they tried it and like it very much.

SUGAR COOKIES

1 cup powdered sugar
1 cup white sugar
1 cup butter
1 cup Crisco
2 eggs
4 cups flour

Mix well. Shape in balls size of a walnut. Place on cookie sheet and press with a glass dipped in sugar. Bake in moderate oven (350°).

Ed Smith from Dagmar spent 20 years in the state legislature. He has also served on many local, state and national boards and commissions. Ed, his wife, Juliet, and two sons run a farm and ranch operation in northeast Montana. He is fondly called Big Ed Smith by his friends and former constituents.

Where you'll always find the best in food, beer, wine and music.

Dear Friends of the Intermountain Children's Home,

While Stavers is famous for it's fine food, and customers are constantly asking for this or that recipe, I thought I would submit to you the following recipe which has never appeared on my menu.

All of us at one time or another are invited to a summer pot luck. This recipe for Broccoli and Grape Salad will be sure to please.

BROCCOLI AND GRAPE SALAD

```
6   ea   Broccoli Stalks
1/2 cup  Sliced Green Onions
1   cup  Diced Celery
2   cup  Red Seedless Grapes, Washed and Dried
4   ozs  Sliced Almonds
1   cup  Raisins
1   lbs  Bacon, Fried Till Crisp and Chopped
              ** Dressing **
1   cup  Good Quality Mayonnaise
1/3 cup  Sugar
1   tbl  White Wine Vinegar
```

1. **Stir the dressing ingredients and set aside.**
2. **Prepare the fruits and vegetables and place in a serving bowl.**
3. **Toss with the dressing and top with the bacon bits and almonds just before serving.**

Although very simple, I've always received compliments.

David Stavers

Stavers Tavern of Hamilton is owned by David Stavers, who is known for serving excellent food. His family has Bitterroot Valley ties that go back to 1916. David's first restaurant, d'Aurias, opened in Hamilton in 1976.

GREEN CHILE BITES

6 eggs, beaten
4 cups grated sharp cheddar cheese
1 4-oz can chopped, mild green chiles
butter

Butter the bottom of an 8x8 inch baking pan. Spread green chilies on bottom of pan. Sprinkle grated cheese over chiles, and pour eggs over all. Bake uncovered at 350 degrees for 30 minutes, or until firm when pan is shaken. Cut in 1 inch squares. Serve hot on a warming tray.

64 pieces

Chili Relleno Casserole

4 7-ounce cans whole, mild green chiles
1 pound Monterey Jack cheese
5 eggs
1$\frac{1}{4}$ cups milk
$\frac{1}{4}$ cup flour
$\frac{1}{2}$ teaspoon salt
   dash of black pepper
4 cups grated mild cheddar cheese (1 pound)

Slit chiles lengthwise on one side. Remove seeds and drain. Slice Monterey Jack cheese into $\frac{1}{4}$-inch thick slices and place inside chiles. Place stuffed chiles in an ungreased 3 quart baking dish. Mix eggs, milk, flour, salt, and pepper well, and pour over chiles. Sprinkle top with grated Cheddar. Bake uncovered at 350 degrees for 45 minutes.

8 servings

Jan Stenerud

Jan Stenerud

Jan Stenerud was recruited to Montana State University from Norway as a skier. Here his kicking skills were discovered and developed for the football program. He played for the Kansas City Chiefs, Green Bay Packers and Minnesota Vikings. He was inducted into the NFL Hall of Fame as the greatest place kicker ever.

STAN STEPHENS
GOVERNOR

BBQ RIBS

1)   Country style ribs with or without bones.   Figure 2-3 ribs per person (plus 2-3 for leftovers)

2)   Bottle of BBQ sauce.   Heinz Original recipe is very good.

3)   1/3-1/2 cup fresh orange juice.

4)   One orange sliced 1/4 inch thick and spread around the ribs.

   Place all this in your crockpot and set on low heat for 8 to 10 hours.   Serve with applesauce and cole slaw.

   These ribs are so good and so easy and better, if possible, the second day. Enjoy!

Stan Stephens was a cable television and broadcast businessman in Havre, and he served 16 years in the State Senate. In 1989, he and his wife, Ann, moved to Helena as he began his term as Montana's 19th governor.

FRESNO STATE UNIVERSITY

BIG WEST CHAMPIONS   •   CALIFORNIA BOWL CHAMPIONS
1977, 1982, 1985, 1988, 1989   1982, 1985, 1988, 1989

JIM SWEENEY'S MONTANA MUD CAKE

Bring to a boil 2 cubes of margarine, 1 cup
water and 4 tablespoons cocoa. Pour into a
mixing bowl and add:

          2 cups flour
          2 cups sugar
          1/2 teaspoon salt

Beat well and add 2 whole eggs, 1/2 cup sour
milk (or cream), 1 teaspoon soda.

Beat well and pour into 18" x 12" cookie
sheet. Bake at 400 degrees for 20 minutes.
While cake is baking, make frosting.

Frosting:

Bring to boil:

          1 stick margarine
          4 tablespoons cocoa
          1/3 cup milk

Add 1 lb. powdered sugar and 1 teaspoon vanilla.
Beat until smooth. Frost while cake is still
warm. Top with chopped nuts if desired.

(Sour milk may be made with 1/2 cup milk and 1
teaspoon vinegar mixed)

"This is the cake I baked for Sister Mary Virginine
at Christian Brothers School" "Sister Virginine
loved chocolate and loved Jim Sweeney"

BULLDOG FOOTBALL Fresno, California 93740 Phone (209) 278-3015 FAX (209) 278-6363

Jim Sweeney coached Butte Central High and Flathead High to five state championships. He was head coach at Montana State University (1963-67) and Washington State (1968-75), with a Rose Bowl victory in 1974. Named coach at Fresno State in 1976, he is the sixth-winningest active college coach in the U.S. He was born and raised in Butte.

Biathlon's Favorite Pre-Race Pasta Dish by Kari Swenson

This recipe was used many times by myself and other biathletes preparing for a big competition.

PESTO PASTA (Basil-Cheese Pasta)

2/3 cup chopped fresh basil leaves
1/3 cup thinly grated fresh Parmesan cheese
1/3 cup olive oil or vegetable oil
2 tablespoons pine nuts or walnuts
1/2 teaspoon salt
1/2 teaspoon pepper
1 clove peeled garlic

Mixed all of the above in a blender until creamy.

Prepare your favorite pasta noodles and add pesto sauce to your own specifications.

I am from Bozeman Montana and began nordic skiing when I was a freshman in high school. I started in the sport of Biathlon after just 2 years of skiing and was named to the Biathlon development team that same year. Biathlon combines the rigors of cross country ski racing and rifle marksmanship into one very interesting sport.

I was a member of the Women's USA Biathlon Team for 7 years during which time I attended 3 World Championships and won many National titles. I brought home a relay bronze medal from the 1984 World Championships in Chamonix France. The 1992 Olympics are the first ever Olympic Games for Women's Biathlon.

I am retired now but know about good nutrition and carbohydrate loading before a race. Have fun and enjoy your pasta!!

Olympic biathlete Kari Swenson was kidnapped and held hostage by two self-styled mountain men in 1984. In a rescue attempt, she was shot and a rescuer friend was killed. Kari's courageous and determined recovery has brought her many awards, a TV movie about the ordeal and a book written by her mother, Victims: The Kari Swenson Story.

Doug Swingley

Iditarod Sled Dog Musher

Simms, Montana

CHERRY CRUNCH

1 can thickened pie cherries

　　SPREAD CHERRIES EVENLY INTO A 9" BAKING DISH, SET ASIDE.

　　　　(pre-heat oven to 350°)

1 cup flour

1 cup sugar

2 tablespoons margarine

1/2 teaspoon salt

1 teaspoon baking powder

1 egg (slightly beaten)

　　BLEND ALL INGREDIENTS IN BOWL WITH A FORK UNTIL CRUMBLY.

SPRINKLE OVER CHERRIES. BAKE 25 MINUTES OR UNTIL LIGHTLY BROWN.

　　CAN BE SERVED WARM WITH CREAM OR ICE CREAM OR COOL.

　　THIS RECIPE WAS GIVEN TO MY WIFE AT THE TIME WE WERE MARRIED

AND IS AN OLD FAMILY FAVORITE. IT IS SIMPLE ENOUGH FOR ANY COOK.

Doug Swingley, together with his brother Greg, raises, trains and races sled dogs. Doug was named Rookie of the Year in the 1992 Iditarod sled race. His goal is to be the first musher from the lower 48 states to win Alaska's Iditarod. He lives in Simms.

THE BLUE ANGELS
UNITED STATES NAVY FLIGHT DEMONSTRATION SQUADRON
Naval Air Station
Pensacola, Florida 32508-7801

STRAWBERRY - BANANA BREAD

ENCLOSED IS A FAVORITE RECIPE WHICH COMES FROM MY WIFE'S SIDE OF
THE FAMILY. NO FAMILY GATHERING WAS CONSIDERED COMPLETE WITHOUT
THE AROMA OF STRAWBERRY-BANANA BREAD FLOATING THROUGH THE HOUSE.
IT IS GUARANTEED TO BE AWESOME!

3 CUPS AND 2 TBSP FLOUR
2 CUPS SUGAR
1 TBSP CINNAMON
1 TSP SALT
1 TSP SODA
1 1/4 CUP CHOPPED PECANS

2 RIPE MASHED BANANAS
4 EGGS - BEATEN
1 1/4 CUP OIL
8 OZ. FROZEN STRAWBERRIES (CHOPPED IN 1/2 OR 1/4'S)

MIX FLOUR, SUGAR, CINNAMON, SALT, SODA AND PECANS IN A BOWL. MIX
BANANAS, EGGS, OIL AND STRAWBERRIES IN A SEPARATE BOWL FIRST AND
THEN MIX WITH OTHER INGREDIENTS. POUR INTO GREASED 7" BY 3 1/2"
PANS (YOU NEED THREE OF THESE) OR 2 5" BY 9" BREAD PANS. SMALLER
PANS WORK BEST. BAKE AT 350 DEGREES FOR 45-50 MINUTES.

MY KIDS REALLY LOVE THIS STUFF. THE KEY IS TO KEEP IT IN THEIR
MOUTHS AND OFF THE FLOOR! ENJOY!

KEN SWITZER
CAPT USMC
BLUE ANGELS
OPPOSING SOLO

Ken Switzer, a graduate of Bozeman Senior High School and the U.S. Naval Academy, was named the National College Boxing Association All-American Boxer in 1982 and 1983. He is also a graduate of the Navy Fighter Weapons School (Top Gun) and is a member of the elite Blue Angels precision flying team, holding the Opposing Solo position.

TILLEMAN MOTOR CO.

Highway 2 West
P.O. Box 2070
Havre, Montana 59501
Telephone 265-7865

CRABMEAT AU GRATIN

1 CUP CHOPPED ONION
1 STALK CELERY,CHOPPED
1/2 CUP BUTTER,MELTED
2 TABLESPOONS CHOPPED GREEN ONION
1/2 CUP ALL-PURPOSE FLOUR
1 13-OZ. CAN OF PET EVAPORATED MILK
2 EGG YOLKS SLIGHTLY BEATEN
1/2 POUND SHREDDED PROCESS
   AMERICAN CHEESE

1 TEASPOON SALT
1 TABLESPOON FRESH MINCED
   PARSLEY
1/2 TEASPOON CAYENNE
   PEPPER
1/2 TEASPOON PEPPER
1 POUND FRESH CRABMEAT

PREHEAT OVEN TO 375 DEGREES. SAUTE' ONIONS, CELERY IN BUTTER OVER LOW HEAT. ADD GREEN ONIONS AND FRY SLIGHTLY. BLEND IN FLOUR, STIRRING WELL. GRADUALLY ADD MILK, AND SEASONINGS, STIRRING CONSTANTLY. COOK UNTIL THICKENED; REMOVE FROM HEAT. GRADUALLY ADD BEATEN EGG YOLKS, STIRRING CONSTANTLY. COOK ON LOW HEAT 5 MINUTES OR UNTIL THICKENED. REMOVE FROM HEAT; GRADUALLY FOLD IN CRABMEAT. POUR MIXTURE INTO A GREASED 1 1/2 QUART CASSEROLE; TOP WITH CHEESE. BAKE AT 375 DEGREES FOR 20 MINUTES. YIELD: 4 SERVINGS.

THIS RECIPE IS ALA- NEW ORLEANS SAINTS ERA (1967-1970) CRAWFISH PEELED OR SHRIMP PEELED CAN BE USED AS SUBSTITUTE TO FRESH LUMP CRABMEAT. THIS RECIPE IS LOW CAL- LOW CHOLESTROL HA! HA! MAKE EXTRA FREEZE AND REHEAT- HAPPY EATING FROM HAVRE,MT !!!

MIKE TILLEMAN

HAVRE,MT

Mike Tilleman played as a defensive tackle for the University of Montana Grizzlies and went on to an 11-year pro football career with the Minnesota Vikings, New Orleans Saints, Houston Oilers and the Atlanta Falcons. From Chinook, he now owns a car dealership in Havre.

J.A. TURNAGE
CHIEF JUSTICE

JUSTICE BUILDING
215 NORTH SANDERS
HELENA, MONTANA 59620-3001
TELEPHONE (406) 444-5490

For nearly forty years, this has been my favorite cake. I do have some difficulty in availability, since Mrs. Turnage reserves the right to prepare the cake on infrequent special occasions!

BOILED RAISIN CAKE

Mix in saucepan and boil together three minutes:

    2 cups raisins
    1-1/2 cups sugar
    1/2 cup shortening
    1 cup water
    1 teaspoon each: cloves, cinnamon, nutmeg
    Pinch of salt

Add 1 teaspoon soda to boiled mixture while hot.

Cool. Add 1 cup water and mix. Add flour for cake consistency--about 2-1/2 cups.

Pour into greased 9 x 13 inch pan. Bake at 325 degrees until done, about 45 minutes.

Frost if desired with cooked brown sugar frosting.

ENJOY!

J. A. Turnage
Chief Justice

Jean Turnage has been Chief Justice of the Montana Supreme Court since 1985. He was president of the Montana State Senate from 1981 to 1983. Born in St. Ignatius, he now lives in Helena.

Office of the President
The University of Montana
Missoula, Montana 59812-1291

(406) 243-2311, FAX (406) 243-2797

FROM THE DENNISON KITCHEN

Clam Chowder
(Serves 6)

2	packages of Knorr's Cream of Mushroom Soup
3	6 oz. cans of chopped clams with liquid
3-4	cups of cooked and cubed potatoes
1	chopped and sauteed onion
2-3	slices of bacon, fried crisp and crumbled
	salt and pepper to taste
2	tablespoons of Sherry
12	ounces of Half-n-Half Milk

DIRECTIONS

Boil and cube potatoes.
Chop and saute onion.
Fry bacon and crumble.
Prepare the Soup according to the instructions on
    the package.
Add potatoes, onion, and bacon and season to taste.
Add clams with liquid, Half-n-Half, and Sherry.
Heat, BUT DO NOT BOIL, just prior to serving,
    stirring well.

SIGNIFICANCE

The Dennison family has traditionally served this tasty Clam
Chowder on Christmas Eve. In 1982, because of a severe Winter
storm, Christmas Eve dinner was very much delayed. One son and his
wife came from Kansas for dinner, but spent all of Christmas Eve in
the airport in Colorado Springs. The other son could not travel
from Denver to Fort Collins -- a distance of just over fifty miles
-- because of the deep snow and terrible road conditions. As a
result, in 1982 the Dennison family had Christmas Eve dinner at
about 3:00, A.M., on the day after Christmas, with one family
member still absent. Nonetheless, the Clam Chowder was marvelous,
as always.

ENJOY!

George M. Dennison
President

STRAWBERRIES & GREEN PEPPERS OVER ICE CREAM

2 TB	BUTTER		1/4 C	WHIPPED CREAM
6 TB	ORANGE JUICE		1 QT	WHOLE HULLED
3 TB	RASPBERRY LIQUEUR			STRAWBERRIES
1/4 C	SMALL DICED GREEN		1 TB	FRESH LEMON JUICE
	BELL PEPPER		1 QT	FRENCH VANILLA ICE
1 TB	ORANGE ZEST			CREAM

Heat butter until it foams. Add orange juice & simmer. Add liqueur. Cook until sauce is slightly thickened. Add green pepper and zest; heat until pepper wilts. Add cream. Taste and adjust flavor with orange juice and liqueur. Add berries and lemon juice.

Scoop ice cream into individual serving dishes; freeze a while to harden the ice cream and frost the dishes. Then turn the warm berries and pepper mixture over ice cream and serve. Serves four.

Strawberries mixed with green peppers served over ice cream! Are we kidding? No way. This peculiar concoction has been a favorite at the **Uptown Cafe'**; you'll be surprised how the peppers complement the strawberries and create an almost chocolatey taste.

At our restaurant, unique dishes are the rule, not the exception. In our seven years of serving lunch and dinner, we have introduced recipes that have inspired many a Montana food lover. In fact, our clientele would be disappointed if we didn't excite their palates with a new dish each time they share a meal with us.

We hope you enjoy the dessert. And please join us in historic Uptown Butte for more of our favorites at Montana's finest restaurant.

Susan Phillips, Guy Graham, and Barb Kornet

The Uptown Cafe, owned by Barbara Kornet, Guy Graham and Susan Phillips, is a very popular Butte restaurant specializing in creative gourmet dinners.

ELEANOR P. VIETOR
Rocking Chair Ranch
Philipsburg, MT

Two favorites:

The cake keeps forever and the older it gets, the better it tastes. I take it to all my business friends as a Christmas greeting.

Wine Cake

1 pkg. yellow cake mix (Betty Crocker)
1 pkg. vanilla pudding mix (not instant)
¾ cup melted butter
4 eggs (not beaten)
¾ cup sherry (Paul Masson pale dry)
1 tsp. nutmeg

Mix all ingredients. Beat with electric beater 5-10 min. I do 10 min.
Bake 40 min. at 375° in angel food type pan.

Hamburger Soup

The soup sits on my stove—pot after pot for lunch all during calving season. We calve in February and March and it hits the spot with dark bread—after a cold morning in the saddle.

Brown 1½ lb. ground beef , add in a large pot
½ cup chopped or thin sliced onion
1½ cup chopped celery
1½ cup thin sliced carrots
2 bay leaves
¼ tsp. thyme
1 tsp. salt
¼ tsp. pepper
1 large can whole tomatoes, crushed
3 cans Swanson's clear broth
3 cans water

If you like mushrooms, slice about 1 cup or 1½ cups and add them. Simmer at least 1 hour. I cool it over night and skim off all fat before reheating.

Eleanor Vietor was born in 1913 and raised on a dude ranch in the Blackfoot Valley east of Missoula. She works as a cowhand on her son's 14,000-acre ranch near Philipsburg. Her tireless energy and love for her work are representative of the true Montana ranchers.

Basic Bio
SYSTEMS, INC.

2837 FORT MISSOULA ROAD
MISSOULA, MONTANA 59801
TEL. (406) 728-0260
FAX (406) 728-0261

To Friends of the Intermountain Children's Home:

This won for me the "Buddy Crocker Cookoff" in 1978, and a "purse" (!) of $1000.

KOORAJIAN's CHEESECAKE

Crust:

1¼ cups of graham cracker crumbs

¼ teaspoon cinnamon

¼ cup sugar

¼ cup melted butter

Mix well and pat into a 9 inch Pyrex pie plate lined with greased aluminum foil.

Filling - First Layer:

1 pound softened cream cheese

½ cup sugar

½ cup eggs (2 large or 3 medium)

3/4 teaspoon vanilla

Beat all ingredients together for 2 - 3 minutes with electric mixer. Pour over crumb crust and bake for 20 minutes @ 375°F. Allow to cool for 15 minutes, then make second layer.

Filling - Second Layer:

1 pint sour cream

¼ cup sugar

1 teaspoon vanilla

Mix and pour over baked first layer. Bake for 10 minutes @ 475°F.

Allow to cool completely and store in refrigerator. VERY RICH!! Serve in small slices. Enjoy....

Bruce

Bruce W. Vorhauer, Ph.D.
President/Chairman

Bruce Vorhauer is owner of Basic Bio Systems in Missoula. He is the inventor of the sponge contraceptive and has a home in the Swan Valley.

101 INTERNATIONAL WAY
POST OFFICE BOX 8182
MISSOULA, MONTANA 59807
TELEPHONE: (406) 523-1300
FAX: (406) 721-4794

This recipe presentation and size of the raviolis were inspired by Mr. Dennis Washington last summer while aboard the *Attessa*. Dennis asked me if raviolis could be made in a way that would allow the flavor of the filling to predominate over the pasta. He told me of a dish that he savored in Tuscany, unlike any tasted before. They were plump and full of flavor, not like the empty tasteless things most people associate with ravioli. We made this recipe to Dennis's specs, the eggs and cream make the filling rich, be quite light and the fresh herbs dance on the palate. The sauce is bursting with fresh flavors and is calorie conscious as well. One word of caution however, you can eat a ton of these! Bon Appetito!!

Bruce Milligan

BASIC PASTA DOUGH

5 LARGE	EGGS	6 Servings
1 POUND	FLOUR	
½ OUNCE	OLIVE OIL	

1. Pour flour into a bowl, add eggs and oil and work together until the dough comes together.

2. Knead for a few minutes, then wrap in plastic and refrigerate for 5 minutes.

3. Remove from refrigerator and cut into long pieces about 6 inches in length and ¼ inch thickness and pass through the rollers of the pasta maker on setting #1. Continue dusting with flour and repeat to #2, #3, #4, #5, until desired thickness is obtained.

4. At this stage you will have a fine sheet that will serve as a lasagna noodle. It may be cut with the other roller to become fettucine or linguine. It can also be cut with a round cutter for tortellini, capeletti or in triangles for agnolotti, squares for ravioli, etc..

5. All pasta should be cooked in an overwhelming amount of salted water. Too little water will result in the pasta becoming pasty and dough like in taste.

WASHINGTON'S FAMOUS VEAL RAVIOLI

1 LB	VEAL (top round, leg, sirloin)
3 OZ	CHEESE (parmesan, romano, asiago)
2 OZ	BREAD CRUMBS
2	EGGS
2 OZ	CREAM (35% or over)
1	SHALLOT CHOPPED
1 CLOVE	GARLIC MINCED
	SALT & PEPPER
TO TASTE	CHOPPED BASIL, SAGE AND PARSLEY (ALL FRESH IF POSSIBLE)

1. Take half of the veal, season and roast in a hot oven 450° for 10 minutes, remove and allow to cool completely.

2. Cut the raw veal and the cooked veal into pieces. In a food processor blend these together until just chunky.

3. Add cheese (grated), bread crumbs, eggs, shallots, garlic, salt & pepper, and herbs.

4. Process until just smooth.

5. Add cream (pulse to combine)

6. Drink Grappa or brandy, you've done a great job so far!

7. Remove from bowl and refrigerate for 1 hour.

8. Take the mixture from refrigerator.

9. Cut pasta sheet into 2 inch or 3 inch squares and with a spoon place enough of the veal mixture into the center of each square (IMPORTANT, most ravioli do not have enough filling in them and you end up eating mostly pasta, this is not the case with "Washington's famous Veal Ravioli's) place enough so that you can just fold the square in half. Moisten the edges of the square with water, fold in half, don't squeeze too hard, the filling should not come to the edges, then crimp the edges with your fingers.

10. After making the ravioli, place them into the large pot of salted boiling water and cook for 4-5 minutes. Remove and cool them under cold water. Oil them so they don't stick together. (This method allows one to prepare in advance then reheat in the same manner just before service.)

SAUCE FOR WASHINGTON'S FAMOUS RAVIOLI

8 OZ	GOOD CHICKEN OR VEAL STOCK
4 OZ	WHITE DRY WINE
	GARLIC, SHALLOT (CHOPPED)
1 LRG	TOMATO (PEELED, SEEDED, FINE SQUARE CUT)
	FRESH BASIL, SAGE, PARSLEY (CHOPPED)
2 OZ	BUTTER
1 OZ	VIRGIN OLIVE OIL

1. in sauce pot, reduce the stock and wine to half in volume.

2. Add chopped garlic, shallot and herbs.

3. Simmer for 1 minute

4. Off the heat, whisk the butter and oil into the sauce, add chopped tomato.

5. Reheat ravioli, strain and place on individual plates in a spiral fashion, spoon the sauce over the pasta, grated fresh parmesan should be sprinkled as well as freshly ground black pepper, garnish with the trio of fresh basil, parsley and sage.

6. Serve with either red or white wine, california chardonnay or Pinot Noir are excellent matches.

Denny Washington founded Washington Construction in 1964. Today the company has expanded into 18 operating entities, including Montana Rail Link and a charitable foundation. The companies are dedicated to high-quality, low-cost service and production. Denny and his wife, Phyllis, live in Missoula.

James Welch
2321 Wylie Street
Missoula, Montana 59802

NEWSPAPER FAKE FONDUE

Preheat the oven to 375 degrees.

8 oz. Swiss cheese, grated medium
1 cup whipping cream
1/2 cup white wine
Day old French bread, cut into 1" cubes
Pinch of cayenne
(Optional: sprinkle of garlic powder)

Fill a well-buttered 1 quart casserole with bread cubes. Combine
rest of ingredients, including cayenne, mix well and pour 1/2
over bread. Allow bread to soak up mixture, then fill again,
allowing plenty of grated cheese to remain on top. Dust with
paprika and bake about 20 minutes, until puffed up and browned.
Serves 3.

Accompany this with a fruit salad.

Note: You can turn today's French bread into day-old bread
cubes by cutting it up and putting fresh cubes on a cookie
sheet in the oven as it heats, as you're grating cheese,
measuring liquids.

My wife, Lois, found this recipe in the Oregonian when she was
teaching at Portland State in the '60s. I was her first
experiment and I loved it. Still do.

*James Welch, born in Browning, is a poet and novelist. Much of the inspiration for his work comes from a Blackfeet/
Gros Ventre background. His latest novel is titled* The Indian Lawyer. *He and his wife, Lois, live in Missoula.*

Office of the President

CHILI WINTER

```
   2  lbs. cubed beef
 1/2  lb. bacon
   1  can (8 oz.) tomato sauce
   1  can (2 lb.) tomatoes, undrained
   2  lb. can kidney beans
   2  lb. can chili beans
   1  green pepper, chopped
   2  onions, chopped
   1  can chopped green chilies
   2  tbs. Worcheshire sauce
8-10  drops tobasco sauce
   1  tsp. chili powder
   1  tsp. cumin
   1  tsp. garlic powder
   1  tsp. black pepper
 1/2  tsp. ground red pepper
   1  can (12 oz.) beer
```

Cook bacon, remove and crumble. Brown cubed meat in bacon
grease. Drain beans and combine all ingredients in a large
kettle and cook for 4 hours. Serve with cornbread.

This is a great meal for a winter day on a "football" Sunday.

W. Michael Easton

W. Michael Easton

Western Montana College
Dillon, Montana 59725

(406) 683-7151
1-800-WMC-MONT

Group A Member

Lones W. Wigger, Jr.
1750 E. Boulder
Colorado Springs, CO   80909
Director, U.S. Shooting Team

I was born and raised on a wheat farm in Montana and became interested in target shooting at a very young age. I attended school at Montana State University, shot on the rifle team there and received my B.S. degree in Agronomy in 1960. After receiving my commission in the U.S. Army through ROTC I went on active duty in 1961 where I remained until my retirement in 1986. While on active duty I spent most of my time with the Army's Marksmanship Unit where I continued to improve my marksmanship skills. I was a member of four Olympic Shooting Teams, winning gold and silver medals in 1964 and a gold in 1972. I am now in charge of the United States Shooting Team located at the Olympic Training Center in Colorado Springs.

Crusty Topped Cauliflower

There is no story behind this recipe other than it is a great way to serve cauliflower.

1 large head fresh cauliflower
1/2 cup mayonnaise
2 teaspoons Dijon mustard
1/2 to 3/4 cup grated Cheddar cheese

In a large pan with a lid, cook cauliflower whole in a small amount of boiling water for about 20 minutes or until tender. Drain well. Place in a flat pan or casserole. Combine mayonnaise and mustard and spread over cauliflower. Sprinkle with cheese. Bake at 350 degrees for 10 minutes or until cheese melts. Serves six.

Lones Wigger, Jr., is from Carter. In 23 years of shooting, he has earned 29 world records, 32 national records, and he won 80 national championships, gold and silver medals in the 1964 Tokyo Olympics and another gold medal in the Olympics at Munich in 1972.

ENTERPRISES

VEGETABLE CASSEROLE

Hank Williams, Jr.

4 T. margarine

4 T. flour

1 1/2 C. milk

1 can Veg-all

1 can asparagus (or use leftover vegetables)

1 T. lemon juice

1/2 t. salt

1/8 t. nutmeg

3 eggs, beaten

grated cheese or buttered bread crumbs

Melt margarine and add flour. Stir and cook until thick. Add milk slowly and stir and cook until thick. Add remaining ingredients and mix. Pour into a 2 quart casserole and top with cheese or bread crumbs.

Bake at 350 degrees for 30 to 40 minutes.

Hank Williams, Jr., son of the country legend, is a successful country western singer. His hits include "All My Rowdy Friends are Coming Over Tonight," and a duet with his father, "There's a Tear in My Beer." He won the 1987-88 Country Music Association Entertainer of the Year award, and a Grammy in 1987. He owns a cabin near Darby and a ranch near Wisdom.

MAJORITY DEPUTY WHIP
———
COMMITTEES:
STEERING AND POLICY
INTERIOR
EDUCATION AND LABOR
CHAIRMAN:
LABOR-MANAGEMENT RELATIONS
SUBCOMMITTEES:
POSTSECONDARY EDUCATION
ELEMENTARY, SECONDARY AND
VOCATIONAL EDUCATION
SELECT EDUCATION
NATIONAL PARKS AND PUBLIC LANDS

PAT WILLIAMS
MONTANA, WESTERN DISTRICT

2457 RAYBURN BUILDING
WASHINGTON, DC 20515-2601
(202) 225-3211

DISTRICT OFFICES:

HELENA 59601
32 N. LAST CHANCE GULCH
(406) 443-7878

BUTTE 59701
FINLEN COMPLEX
(406) 723-4404

MISSOULA 59802
302 WEST BROADWAY
(406) 549-5550

Congress of the United States
House of Representatives
Washington, DC 20515-2601

THE BUTTE PASTY
(pass-tee)

PASTRY:
3 cups flour
1/2 to 1 teaspoon salt
1 1/4 cups lard or shortening
3/4 cup very cold water

Measure flour and salt. Cut in lard until dough resembles small peas. Add water and divide into 6 equal parts.

FILLING:
5 or 6 medium potatoes (red are best)
3 medium or 2 large yellow onions
Parsley for flavoring
2 pounds of meat
(loin tip, skirting or flank steak)
butter
salt and pepper

Roll dough slightly oblong. Slice in layers on dough, first the potatoes, then the onions and last the meat -- sliced or diced in thin strips. Bring pasty dough up from ends and crimp across the top. Making the pasty oblong eliminates the lump of dough on each end. Bake at 375 degrees for about one hour. Brush a little milk on top while baking.

NOTE: Old-timers claim the pasty arrived in Butte, Montana along with the first housewives who followed their husbands into the mining camp. Long favored in the copper miner's lunch bucket, the pastry-wrapped meal was an ideal way for "Cousin Jeannie" to provide a hearty meal for the hard-working "Cousin Jack." As the miner unwrapped his lunch, he would refer to the pasty as a "letter from 'ome." Its popularity spread quickly throughout the camp, and today the pasty is as much a part of Butte as the Berkeley Pit.

-- from the Butte Heritage Cookbook --

Pat Williams began representing Montana's Western Congressional District in the U. S. House of Representatives in 1978. He has served four terms as a Majority Deputy Whip for the House Democratic leadership. Williams was born in Helena and raised in Butte.

Bonnie J Ranch
STAR ROUTE 1 BOX 155 ⚫ TROUT CREEK, MONTANA 59874

Jimme & Eileen Wilson

563 Spaghetti Sauce

2 lbs. lean ground beef
1 (29 oz.) can tomato sauce
1/2 cup ketchup
1 cup water
1 medium onion, chopped
2 (4 oz.) cans mushroom bits & pieces
1 tbsp. Worcestershire sauce
1 tsp. chili powder
1 pinch ground cloves
1 pinch oregano
1 pinch garlic powder
Salt & peper

Step #1. Brown ground beef & chopped onions.
Step #2. Drain off excess fat.
Step #3. Add tomato sauce, ketchup, water and seasonings.
Step #4. Add mushroom bits & pieces.
Step #5. Cook at low-moderate heat for 1 hour.

The sauce got its name from a high-spirited animal (ID #563) we were feeding for locker beef. One day he jumped out of the pen where he was confined and injured himself. We had to put him in the freezer a little earlier than anticipated. After that, every package of meat was referred to as "old 563."

Jimme Wilson, a native of Billings, is the first Montanan to serve as president of the National Cattlemen's Association. Jimme and his family operate a registered commercial Hereford cattle ranch near Trout Creek in northwest Montana.

I am not a good cook. But I am a great eater... darn
good eater. There is nothing better than stopping by the R.
B. Murrays' place near Cascade for Mrs. Murray's cheese
crackers. They are made with soft cheese and are best eaten
when one sits by the Missouri River at sunset. My mother in
Great Falls cooks as if dinner was art. It looks as good as
it tastes... and it tastes swell. Oh, and the pie at
Gamer's in Butte... it is the kind where the crust breaks
off in warm layered chunks and the berries melt the ice
cream right on the fork.

To write all of the above about great cooks in Montana
(the Dinner State), is designed to delay me having to
mention my best recipe... which is the task I was asked to
do. None of my long tradition of eating in Montana rubbed
off on my cooking. My cooking barely rubs off plates even
when scalded to hundreds of degrees in the heavy duty cycle
of a dishwasher. For as a bachelor cook, I am even a
disgrace to fellow horrible bachelor cooks who, when away
from visits to Mom, also dine from the two basic food groups
(Dorito Chips and Chips-A-Hoy Cookies).

In fact, the only recipe I know is already printed on the
side of the Instant Potato Bud box. You take a semi-clean
dish, pour some potato flakes in it, wipe a finger tip full
of yellow stuff from the tub-o-margerine (first, check to
see that the expiration date occurred within at least the
last decade), pour in enuff water so the flakes drown, put
it all in the microwave, and pull it out when you can smell
it through the vents on top... or until there are clouds in
the little window. Eat it until you can't move any of it in
the dish.

Obviously, this isn't what the fine folks at the classy
Montana Magazine wanted for their cookbook. So, I asked a
friend, Janet Thomas for the recipe she uses for her cold
Salmon. She cooks good enough to be an Montanan, even
though she isn't. She has never been to Montana, but I am
sure she would like it, so her recipe deserves to be here.
I call it Big Sandy Cold Poached Salmon because I don't
think any food has been named after Big Sandy, and every
town deserves a good dish named after it. Janet tells me
the recipe is originally from Bon Appetit Magazine. That
must be a good magazine... as this is good.

BIG SANDY COLD POACHED SALMON (with dill stuff on it)
Serves six or five (if I am there)

The stuff you gotta buy, the sauce, and what you do with it
all follows on the next page.

ABC Entertainment 4151 Prospect Avenue Hollywood CA 90027 (213) 557 5988

GOOD MORNING AMERICA

```
FISH STUFF
2 quarts water
1 medium sliced onion
1/4th cup fresh lemon juice
10 whole black peppercorns
2 teaspoons salt
2 bay leaves
6 1-inch thick salmon steaks

SAUCE STUFF
1 cup mayonnaise
1/4th cup buttermilk
2 tablespoons chopped fresh dill or 2 teaspoons dried
dillweed
1 tablespoon minced fresh parsley
2 teaspoons fresh lemon juice
1 teaspoon grated lemon peel
1 mall garlic clove, pressed

A few lemon slices
Janet also uses something that looks like dill trees with
their trunks cut off... I think they are called sprigs.

For the fishies: Bring the first 6 ingredients (that's all
the first stuff except the fish themselves) to boil in a
large heavy saucepan.  You don't want the pot to bust over
the flame.  Reduce the heat, cover and simmer 30 minutes.
Add 3 salmon steaks to saucepan and simmer just until cooked
through, about 6 minutes.  Transfer to plate using slotted
spatula.  Repeat cooking technique with remaining 3 salmon
steaks.  Cover and refrigerate salmon until chilled, about 2
hours.  During this time, you can wonder why recipe writers
never use complete sentences.  (Can be prepared 1 day
ahead).

For the sauce: Mix all the stuff under the Sauce list
(except the lemon slices and the dill trees), in a small
bowl.  Cover and chill at least one hour.  (Can be prepared 1
day ahead)

Top salmon steaks with lemon slices and dill sprigs (trees)
Invite me over, and serve with sauce.
```

Craig Wirth, an Emmy winner, is a reporter for ABC's Good Morning America, *a reporter for NBC's cable division (CNBC) and a feature reporter for KTVX-TV in Salt Lake City. He grew up in Great Falls.*

BIG SKY FILMS

2200 E. EDGEWOOD DRIVE; WHITEFISH, MT 59937

B.J.'s TENDER SALMON

This recipe was formulated in self-defense, after being served too many dry and overcooked salmon dinners. Salmon has a delicate flavor and supple texture, both of which can be obliterated by excessive exposure to heat. For succulent medallions of tender salmon please try this tasty home remedy.

3 Tablespoons of Butter (or Margarine)
1 Tablespoon of Lemon Juice
1 Teaspoon minced Garlic
1 Pinch of dried Dill Weed
4 Salmon Steaks (approx. 1 inch thick)
4 Wedges of fresh Lemon

Set the oven on Broil, and allow to pre-heat.

Lightly coat bottom of a 9 by 13 inch glass pan with vegetable oil.

Combine butter, lemon juice, garlic and dill weed in small sauce pan. Heat mixture until butter melts, then stir together and set aside.

Wash salmon steaks thoroughly and pat dry.

Baste both sides of steaks with ½ of prepared mixture, and place them in glass pan. Place glass pan in oven so that steaks are approximately 2 inches from broiler burner. Cook for 6 minutes. Baste both sides of steaks again, and turn steaks over. Cook for another 6 minutes; check for doneness. Salmon is ready when flakes at center of steaks are barely cooked. If additional cooking is desired, please do so 1 minute at a time. Do not overcook!

Garnish with lemon wedges and enjoy.

B J Worth

B. J. Worth

B.J. Worth won four World Skydiving Aerobatics titles. Beginning with the James Bond film Moonraker, *he has coordinated all of the aerial stunts and performed some of the major ones for each Bond film. B.J. is stunt coordinator for television's* Stunt Masters. *He is a University of Montana graduate and has a home in Whitefish.*

United States Department of the Interior

NATIONAL PARK SERVICE
YELLOWSTONE NATIONAL PARK
WYOMING 82190

IN REPLY REFER TO:

More times than I can remember I have sprung surprise lunch guests on my wife Carol. Corn chowder with bread sticks or corn bread has been a consistent favorite to bail me out.

Robert D. Barbee

Southwestern Corn Chowder

Makes 8 cups

6 slices bacon
1 medium onion chopped (3/4 cup)
1/4 lb. mushrooms, sliced (or 4 oz. can)
1 large potato, diced (1 1/2 cup)
1/2 c. water
1 can (17 oz.) cream style corn
1 can mushroom soup
2 cups milk
1 tsp. salt
1 can (4 oz.) diced green chilies

Cook bacon until crisp. Drain and crumble. Stir fry onion, mushrooms and potato in 2 Tbsp. bacon fat for 3 to 5 minutes. Add water, cover, and simmer for 10 minutes. Add rest of ingredients and bring to a boil. Reduce heat. Add bacon and simmer for 10 minutes. Best made early so flavors can blend.

Yellowstone National Park, 2,219,823 acres large, is the nation's and the world's oldest national park. Thermal features and abundant wildlife amidst magnificent scenery are its major drawing points.

YOGO CREEK SUPREME

INGREDIENTS

FISHING POLE AND BAIT
A COUPLE HOURS OF TIME
CAMP FIRE
CAST IRON FRY PAN
CORN MEAL
LITTLE OIL
SALT AND PEPPER TO TASTE

Clean and prepare fresh pan size brookies caught from Yogo Creek. Get camp fire ready.

Roll fish in corn meal – place in hot oil in cast iron fry pan over the camp fire. Cook until golden brown and a little crispy.

An added accent to this meal is raw fried potatoes prepared over the camp fire.

The miners enjoy going fishing after a long hard days work in the mine.

VORTEX MINING
SPECIALIZING IN YOGO SAPPHIRES
UTICA. MT

CHUCK & MARIE RIDGEWAY – LANNY & JOY PERRY – PETE ECKER

Yogo sapphires are known for their incredible uniformity of rich blue colors and virtual absence of flaws. These precious gems were discovered in 1894 near Utica in Yogo Gulch.

INDEX